Things *I Want My* Kids *to Know About* Money

SIMPLE HACKS FOR FINANCIAL SUCCESS

MIKE IBEN

ISBN: 978-0-578-38427-6 (Paperback)

Front cover image by Tanja Prokop of TLI Design.
Book edited by Jessica Cornwell of Jessica Cornwell Author Services.

Printed in the United States of America.

First printing edition 2022.

Mike Iben
Iben Thinking LLC
IbenThinkingLLC@gmail.com

To Jen, Cate & Grace

Contents

Chapter 1
What's This All About?

Like most parents with two teenagers, you wonder if you have done an adequate job all these years fully preparing them for the real world. And you wonder why they take so long in the bathroom, but that's for a different book. Teenagers worry about friends, schoolwork, social media status updates, and their social calendars. But you know that very soon, things will start to get very real for them. As you get older, the world brings big responsibilities that include their own jobs, committed relationships or marriages, their own kids, bills to pay, savings to make, and the ups and downs of life.

As parents, we do our best to teach our kids about dangers such as drinking, drugs, and sex. We teach our kids about showing respect for each other and making a positive impact on the world. We teach our kids about the value of an education. But for some reason we often miss the lessons about money. And that is a BIG miss. Households in the United States increasingly experience higher amounts of debt, lower retirement savings, and less education about how to manage finances. Over-spending could be considered an epidemic.

My parents rarely talked to me about money and I would guess the same was true with their parents. It's not as if they were intentionally withholding information; they just didn't know any better. I had a great childhood where we had everything we needed and rarely went without.

In our society, talking about finances and wealth among close friends and relatives can be uncomfortable and seems taboo. If someone is doing well, they do not want to speak up for fear of bragging. If someone is struggling, they shy away from asking for help or advice for fear of shaming. No one wants to admit mistakes or a lack of knowledge on any level, but especially when it comes to money.

> **Knowledge Drop**
>
> According to Debt.org, the average American household has 2.7 credit cards with an average household debt of $5,315.

Also, the real-life skills of money management are not a required curriculum in many of our schools. An education at every level should provide knowledge so our kids are prepared to be outstanding adults who contribute to society. By not requiring them to learn and understand money basics, we are withholding a key piece of knowledge for success.

So where do we turn for financial advice?

I have very few instances where money was part of a conversation with my parents, and those instances were not deep conversations by any means. When I was around eight, my father sold a lawn mower to one of our neighbors. Part (or all) of the payment was a $100 bill. He let me hold the bill in my hands. I was mesmerized by it because I had never seen one before. I held it up and stared at it long enough that my father began to laugh at me.

As the world evolves, most money now changes hands electronically which makes it harder for us to teach our children about the value of money. Let your kids see and touch coins and bills and talk about the value of each. Have you ever seen the terror in a teenage cashier's eyes when they are forced to make change after your purchase at the local convenience store? Have you seen the impatient rage in a customer's face in the same scenario? Kids need to learn about the value of money from somewhere, so why not from the adults in their lives?

In my early teens, I asked my mother if we were rich. Her response was, "We are comfortable." I still don't know what that means other than we had everything we "needed," not necessarily everything we "wanted." Later in life I found out my parents had filed bankruptcy somewhere along the way and they never had the ability or knowledge to save much of anything.

When I was in my mid-teens, I had a bad run-in about money with my father. As is typical with teenagers, I was becoming more independent with my thinking, which in common speak means I was acting arrogant, spoiled, and unappreciative. Leading up to Christmas that year, I overheard several conversations where my parents were complaining about not having enough money. Some of the discussions were directed at me, but most were amongst themselves.

Most years, my parents allowed me to open a Christmas present a day or two before the rest of the family arrived. (Side note: I was the youngest child by nine years, so all my siblings had moved away by this time. As my mother explained the number of years between me and my next oldest sibling, "We were not expecting you, but once we had you, we really liked you." Good talk, Mom.) On this Christmas, my mom and dad allowed me to open TWO presents before the regular Christmas present opening ceremony took place. The presents were an Intellivision (which was a state-of-the-art video game console for its time) and a small TV to play it on. Pretty awesome gifts! My response? Did I jump up and hug them both saying how much I loved them? Nope. Did I thank them profusely and ask which chores I could do to show my appreciation? Nope. Did I sit there on my ass with a scowl on my face

Knowledge Drop

According to Wikipedia, Intellivision sold 3 million consoles from 1980 to 1983 and IGN ranked it No. 14 of the greatest video game consoles of all time.

while saying, "I thought we didn't have any money? Why did you buy these things if we don't have enough money?" Yep.

Now, let me say my father was a very loving person who taught me a lot about life. He grew up working on the family farm (which was an obligation), fought in World War II (where he volunteered at seventeen), and worked six days per week during my entire childhood, and when he got mad, the world stopped turning, if you know what I mean. My comments understandably caused him to take notice and he felt the need to counsel me. He brought his wrath down on me like no other time I had ever seen. While utilizing several words I had never heard him use before, he basically said, "I am never buying you anything ever again!" When I think back with regret over that day, I must remind myself that a teenage mind is far from being fully developed.

I did not understand the value of money, how hard my parents worked for it, or why they spent money when they said they could not afford to.

The value of money is tough to teach because it can be tied to emotion – the emotion of wanting something you cannot have, afford, or need. We live in a world of FOMO (fear of missing out) through social media reporting lavish vacations, expensive meals, parties you were not invited to, and people leading a life supposedly better than yours. Money and wealth provide you and your family opportunities to achieve the experiences that are important to you. Along the way, it can also cause anxiety, uncertainty, and frustration.

A good financial plan should start with focusing on you and your family, not what others have. Nobody cares how much money you have, so why should you covet that of others? Focus on *your* financial goals and things will fall into place.

If money is used properly, you can achieve your personal and financial goals. If it is not used properly, your goals may never be achieved and the repercussions of severe mismanagement of money could last an entire lifetime.

When our youngest daughter was still in diapers, I woke up in a panic one day telling my wife that we needed to develop lesson plans for our kids. My wife was a teacher during that time, so lesson plans for the classroom were a standard process. For whatever reason, on that day I was concerned about capturing a complete and comprehensive list of everything we needed to teach our kids. Have I told you I am detail-oriented, and some would say anal? (Not to my face, but I know they say it.) Missing some key topic to teach made me nervous and anxious because it is our job to prepare these little people to enter the real world.

So, this book is primarily for our kids in hopes of giving them tools to manage money properly. The information in this book (lesson plans) can be used as teaching tools for kids or useful tips as adults. Either way, the content in this book will help create a better understanding of money right now. My kids are teenagers and I want to use this material as a guide for them to build a good financial foundation, but I also want our kids to keep this as a reference guide into the future as they go to college, start a career, and build a family of their own. With that said, I also hope this book can be used by anyone wanting to learn more about their money. If it helps anyone become a better manager of their money and have better control over their financial stability, then I will claim success.

ABOUT THE BOOK

What the book WILL offer

Through a long series of small, disciplined financial decisions during our lives, my wife and I have been able to meet our financial goals. Our financial success is self-made, meaning we did it without an inheritance, lottery winnings, or any other influx of money that was not related to our hard work and money decisions. We have been blessed and fortunate to have excellent educations, great jobs, opportunities to advance

Money Decree
Building wealth is a series of small, disciplined decisions.

financially, and we have lived in good health. But those alone will not make you wealthy.

This book details many of those decisions, tools, and techniques that got us where we are today. I grew up in a lower middle-class family, paid my own way through a state college, began my professional career with student debt, and struggled to make ends meet, like many families in this country.

This book provides real-world, day-to-day examples of how to manage your money. I have provided a plethora of those decisions, tools, and techniques – financial hacks, if you will – that helped us build wealth and become financially independent. They are financial hacks any person can do on their own for little or no cost, other than time and effort. The book includes big time hacks like how to buy a house (Chapter 30) or car (Chapter 29) without going into insurmountable debt, evaluating a job offer (Chapter 9) or identifying how much money to save and where to save it (Chapters 14, 15, 16). But it also includes more simplistic hacks like how to make the best of your Costco membership (Chapter 27), ways to reduce expenses just by balancing your bank statements (Chapter 23), and how not to get stiffed at happy hour (Chapter 28).

My goal is also to provide you knowledge about things like how loans are structured, types of insurance you need, how to take full advantage of workplace benefits programs, and how to use credit cards to your advantage. Additionally, definitions for common financial terms will be provided along the way and in a reference section in the back of the book.

What the book will NOT offer

I am not a financial advisor, investment manager, certified public accountant, or any other type of professional in the financial industry. All the details provided are offered as guidance to help you manage your finances better through decision-making, tools, and techniques we have used in our adult lives.

This book is not necessarily to help you get out of excessive debt, but to help you not get there in the first place. Additionally, this is not a book about how to invest in the stock market or other securities, but rather how to put yourself in a position to invest in the stock market or other securities to effectively build wealth and improve your financial security.

How the book is structured

The book is written in six parts, with the first four providing guidance on developing solid financial plans through good decision-making, and the last two are reference sections, as described below.

Part I: The Purpose of Money

We'll provide a foundation and discuss the meaning of wealth and what it requires to achieve it.

Part II: Making Money

Focus on the income side of the wealth equation.

Part III: Saving Money

Discover how to save a larger part of your income.

Part IV: Spending Money (Or Not)

Investigate tools and techniques to spend money efficiently and with purpose.

Part V: A Bunch of Helpful Lists

Observe a financial calendar of action items throughout the year and other lists referenced throughout the book.

Part VI: Definitions

This reference section provides the definition of common financial terms referenced throughout the book.

Some of the financial terms defined in this book may seem remedial to some of you. I promise I am not trying to insult anyone's intelligence here. I have approached these definitions (and the book) the same way I teach my teenagers how to drive – I am not taking anything for granted and I assume they know nothing. You don't want your kids touching the gas pedal until they know how to use the brake. I will define most everything, even if it turns out to be remedial. My goal is to ensure everyone knows these financial terms and I am not assuming anything.

Now, with the foundation set, let me share the *Things I Want My Kids to Know About Money*.

PART I

THE PURPOSE OF MONEY

Chapter 2

The Financial Pyramid

Like most anything else, money is easier to manage when you have a goal and a plan for where you are going. For example, if you are taking a cross country road trip with your family, planning is vital. Which roads will be most conducive for your travel? Do you want to take backroads to see the largest ball of twine, or stay on the interstate and get to your destination as quickly as possible? How large (or small) is your spouse's bladder? Where will you stay along the way? How many miles will you drive each day? Will you stop to eat or take food along in the car? This vacation is exhausting already, and we haven't even left yet. And for some reason, my wife is no longer speaking to me.

Add a component such as a global pandemic and it makes the plan even more complicated. Where will we be able to find an open restaurant? Will we be able to sit down inside or use the drive-through? Which gas stations will be open? Where are public restrooms open and available? Do we have enough hand sanitizer?

To achieve goals, you need to have plans. The great news is the following pages will help you develop AND execute your financial plans. The starting point of plan building is understanding where you currently are compared to where you want to go. To start that process, let us discuss the illustration below that I have dubbed the

"Financial Pyramid." The Financial Pyramid helps identify your current state of financial health.

FINANCIAL PYRAMID

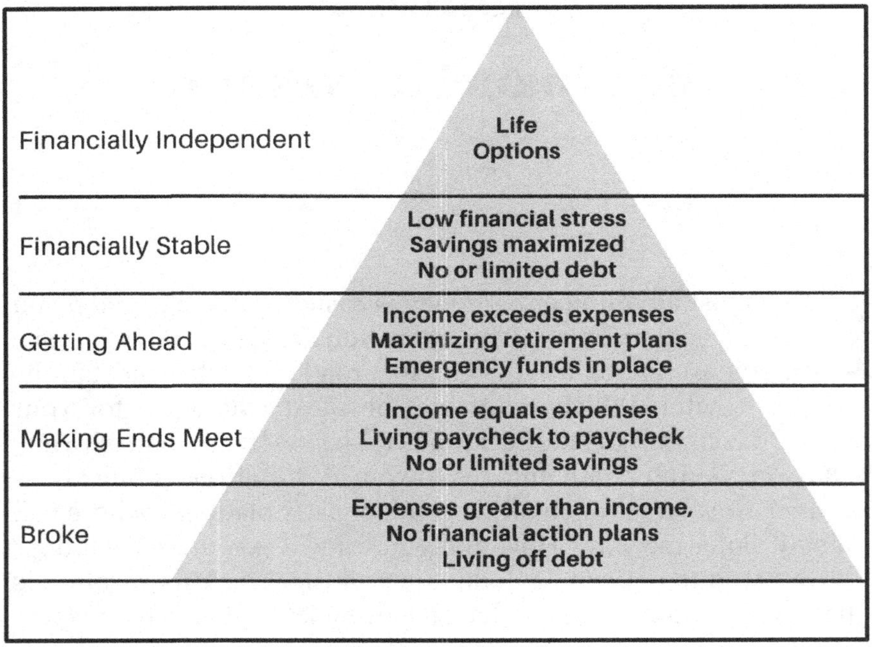

As you can see, the Financial Pyramid has five levels of financial health, starting at the bottom with being broke and ending at the top with being financially independent. Each level has common characteristics of financial well-being, but no person will fit neatly in any one level. As you review the characteristics, visualize which level you have most in common with your current financial situation, knowing that you may have the characteristics in multiple levels.

Let's break down each level so you can establish where you are currently, identify where you want to be in the near term, and then your goal for a longer span of time. Many terms used in this section such as net worth, emergency funds, and credit scores will be discussed and defined in greater detail in the coming chapters, but you can always utilize the reference section at the end of the book to define terms unclear to you.

Broke

A person or family who is broke is in financial dire straits and cannot survive over a long period without significant changes in their financial health. Other characteristics may include:

- Expenses are greater than their income.
- There are no emergency funds, savings accounts, or retirement funds.
- They are living off an increasing amount of debt, most likely created by using credit cards.
- Bills are regularly not paid on time.
- They have poor credit scores.
- A missed paycheck is immediately catastrophic.
- They have negative net worth.

Making Ends Meet

A person or family who is making ends meet generally can pay their ongoing expenses and take care of their needs to live, but little else. Other characteristics may include:

- Income and expenses are equal.
- There are few or no emergency funds, savings accounts, or retirement funds.
- They use credit cards for emergencies and monthly expenses that are higher than normal.
- They have higher debt than they are able to pay off in a reasonable amount of time.
- Bills are generally paid on time.
- They have average credit scores.

- A missed paycheck can be viable for only a short period of time, if at all.
- They have negative or low net worth.

Getting Ahead

A person or family who is getting ahead can reasonably cover their expenses and have money set aside for future needs. Other characteristics may include:

- Income exceeds expenses.
- Emergency funds are in place, and savings and retirement accounts are utilized with all available funds.
- Credit cards are used strategically and paid off each month.
- Size of debt is manageable.
- Bills are always paid on time.
- They have above average credit scores.
- A missed paycheck is not catastrophic.
- They have positive and increasing net worth.

Financially Stable

A person or family who is financially stable has their financial house in order. They understand how to use money effectively and are on a path to achieve future financial goals. Other characteristics may include:

- Income exceeds expenses.
- Emergency funds and savings accounts are fully funded. Retirement accounts are maximized according to tax limits. Balances are above average according to age and number of years to retirement.
- If credit cards are used, they are used strategically and paid off each month.
- They have little or no debt. All debt is strategic in its purpose.
- Bills are always paid on time.

- They have excellent credit scores.
- A missed paycheck is not catastrophic.
- They have high net worth for age and number of years to retirement.

Financially Independent

A person or family who is financially independent has achieved all or most of their financial goals. They no longer need to work to live out their life ambitions. They understand how to use money effectively to achieve current and future financial objectives. Other characteristics may include:

- Income from a regular paycheck is not needed to cover expenses.
- Emergency funds are fully funded. Savings and retirement accounts are fully funded and provide enough income to meet short-term and long-term needs.
- Credit cards are used strategically and paid off each month, if used at all.
- They have little or no debt. All debt is strategic in its purpose.
- Bills are always paid on time.
- They have excellent credit scores.
- They have high net worth for age and number of years to retirement.

The information in this book will help you no matter your location on the Financial Pyramid. My hope is to teach my kids - and maybe you and your kids too - enough about money that they will be fortunate enough to not fall into financial dire straits and be consistently broke over a long period of time. However, life happens, and many times things cannot be controlled. If you or a loved one ends up in a financial catastrophe, numerous reputable resources and information can be found online that include http://www.usa.gov/debt or www.consumer.ftc.gov. I have also found the information offered by Dave Ramsey provides excellent advice about using sound financial practices.

So where do you stand on the Financial Pyramid? Are you happy with where you are financially? If the answer is yes, then congratulations! But what's next?

If the answer is no, what are you willing to do to get where you want to be? Reading this book is an excellent way to start or continue on a path to your financial goals. With that said, money is not everything and should not determine your whole life. A satisfying life is achieved by doing the things you value with the people you love.

Money Decree
Put an emphasis on experiences instead of material things.

Money gives you freedom and independence to make the choices you want in life instead of others making them for you, but you must determine what that means for you and your family.

Now that you have an understanding of your financial health and where you currently fit on the Financial Pyramid, take the next step in establishing where you want to go by asking yourself these questions. Write your answers on a piece of paper:

- What are some activities I value but cannot fully participate in as much as I would like because of my current financial health?
- What do I want the latter part of my life to look like? Do I want to retire, travel, own a vacation home, or start my own business?
- How much am I willing to sacrifice in the short term to achieve my long-term goals?

You now have goals. They are real goals because you wrote them on a piece of paper. And I will assume that most of you have a dream of being at or near the top of the Financial Pyramid by achieving financial independence.

Keep your goals in a place where you will be reminded of them on a regular basis. When I make goals, I usually put recurring reminders in my calendar to go look at them and make sure I am staying on pace for success. For example, every month I have a reminder pop up to look at this year's resolutions I committed to in January. It holds me accountable throughout the year and provides validation that I am anal. Supposedly. Over time I have found this system works for me, but it may not be good for everyone. Find one that works for you and helps guide you toward successfully meeting your goals.

> **Knowledge Drop**
>
> It is estimated that the great pyramid in Giza took 23 years to build. How long will it take you to build yours? Financial Pyramid that is.

Your financial goals are no different than having goals to eat better, drink less, exercise more, or read new books. We all need regular motivation and accountability. But also know that we sometimes fall off the wagon. That's okay. Stay focused on your goals (even when you have the occasional lapse) and you can keep moving up the Financial Pyramid.

Moving up the Financial Pyramid can sometimes be hard and feel insurmountable. It takes time and a commitment to achieve the life of which you dream.

Every person who achieved their goal of running a marathon started by running some distance much shorter than 26.2 miles; maybe they started by running only a hundred yards.

Every person who achieved their goal of losing fifty pounds started by losing their first pound before achieving their ultimate goal.

Every person who achieved their goal of a college education started by attending their first class.

Every self-made millionaire started by saving a dollar. The time to start saving your dollar is now.

Chapter 3

There are NO Shortcuts

The tools shared within this book are habits and fundamentals I learned over my 50+ years of life. They are tools that *anyone* can use. In fact, they are tools that everyone *should* use to move up the Financial Pyramid and ultimately on a path of financial independence.

When I was in my late twenties, I told my wife about a big financial goal of mine. I told her when I got to my mid-fifties, I wanted to have a choice of whether I continued to work. Basically, I was saying I wanted us to have enough money to become financially independent by then. By following through on my financial goals year in and out, I was able to become financially independent ahead of schedule, when I was 48.

Our financial success has come from good financial habits and sound money management. Along the way, my wife and I have had times of financial soundness and peace of mind. This included great paychecks, running a successful mid-sized business, and selling that business for a significant profit. The bad times included being laid off twice – once during the Great Recession. But through it all, we stuck to our core habits to manage our money.

Money Decree
Do not buy into get-rich-quick schemes. Buying a lottery ticket is not a retirement plan.

The sale of our business certainly helped on our path to financial independence, but it was not necessarily required. Even before owning a business, we were on our way to the goal of financial independence by our mid-fifties. I tell you this to prove a couple of important points.

First, a sudden windfall of money is unlikely or at least rare, and you should never plan for it. If winning the lottery is your plan for retirement, then you need a new plan. If you are counting on a huge inheritance from your relatives, think again. If you think your taxes will fully fund a government-provided retirement, you are mistaken.

There are no quick ways to become rich and you should run away if someone tells you differently. The best way to financial independence is to create excellent financial habits and stick to your goals day in and day out.

Secondly, even if you are fortunate enough to receive a large financial windfall, you still need to manage it prudently. A windfall is not an endless supply of money. Receiving a windfall can cause a frenzy of uncontrolled spending, especially if you have no financial planning.

No matter how much money you receive by way of a paycheck or a lottery ticket, you need to manage that money properly in order to make it last. There are no shortcuts!

Chapter 4

Start Learning About Money TODAY (And Never Stop)

I grew up in a household that didn't talk about money or know how to use it in our best interest. My guess is my parents couldn't teach me much about money because they didn't know themselves - probably because no one ever taught them. Both my parents worked hard and earned a fair wage. They provided a nice home, food on the table, and a great childhood filled with lifelong memories. Fortunately, we did not go without any needs.

However, later in my childhood I found out that my mom and dad had filed bankruptcy at some point. I don't know the circumstances, but I'm sure it was an incredible hardship on them. They rebounded nicely, but as they got older and transitioned out of the job market, they didn't have any sort of nest egg and lived off Social Security for the rest of their lives. For a number of years, they lived in a house my sister owned and paid rent well below the market. My wife and I would commonly buy them plane tickets to visit because we knew they could not afford them otherwise. In fact, I had found out they borrowed money from another sibling to drive from Iowa out to Arizona on one occasion. They had great lives surrounded by friends in a town they lived most of their lives, but if they had greater financial resources, I have no doubt they would have lived their lives a bit differently.

Fortunately, over the years I learned the ins and outs of money from some influential nonfamily members in my life and by reading about the topic. For whatever reason, I remember being a tight ass pretty much my whole life. I liked to spend money as much as the next person, but I enjoyed saving it more.

Back in 1981, I traveled on an airplane for the very first time to Anaheim, California with my parents for a vacation. After we returned, I found out the plane ticket cost around $300, so I put an immediate plan in place to begin earning $1 per day so I could buy another plane ticket. Since I was twelve years old, my earning potential was limited to working for my dad at a lumber yard, mowing lawns and babysitting, so saving $1 per day was a bit aggressive. When my mom heard about my plans, she responded by saying, "Good luck with that." With her strong motivational speech, I started my plan to save. I was able to save some money, but not $300. I didn't think through the fact that my family wouldn't have let me go by myself anyway, or that the cost of a plane ticket was only a slice of the financial pie of funds it takes to go on vacation.

This was probably the first major financial goal I set for myself, and I had no concept of how to get there. The goal was not realistic because I was restricted on my earning potential, and even if I would have saved $300, it wasn't enough for the trip in the first place. Setting goals is crucial in the process but understanding if the goal is reasonable and identifying the key steps toward success are equally important. Just saying you want to move up the financial pyramid is not enough. What steps are you going to take to get there? Those steps need to include learning the best ways to accomplish your goal.

Learning never stops for any topic, but it is especially true about money. Over a lifetime, many financial changes happen. Goals for your money change. When you are a child, you save up to buy a candy bar or bag of chips. When you are a teenager, you save up to have an In-N-Out Burger with your friends or to buy a new pair of jeans at the mall. Over time, your attention shifts to starting and supporting a family, college funding, and retirement. The older you get, the more complicated money can become because of all the things that can drain your financial resources, such as rent, groceries, utilities, car payments, dining out, and other bills. It is critically important to continually learn how to utilize your money in your best interest, no matter your financial goal.

Learning topics should include the best ways to budget, spend money, save money, invest money, build wealth, and reduce tax exposure. Great sources for money information can be found in the business section of your local newspaper, the Money section of USA Today, or finance sections of various news websites. Find personal finance books at your local library. Research dependable radio shows or podcasts that discuss everyday money topics, however, you should be careful about the motivation of the speaker or premise of the podcast. Stay away from infomercials that want you to buy into a program and promise quick results. Are they trying to sell you a get-rich-quick scheme or to buy into investments? Do they guarantee to reduce your debt quickly and without effort? If so, steer clear. Stick with people or organizations that teach tried and true conservative money concepts. There are several great options, but a good one to listen to would be Dave Ramsey. While I do not agree with all his advice, he offers excellent resources and discussion topics which help gain financial knowledge.

Chapter 5

Being Rich Means Something Much Different Than People Think It Does

I read an article once that had a powerful statement relating to money and wealth. The statement said something to the effect of "Most people who say they want to be millionaires *actually* mean they want to *spend* a million dollars, which is the exact opposite of being a millionaire." I found this to be powerful for a few reasons. First, most people have a hard time distinguishing between income and wealth. Second, we live in a consumer-driven society where there is incredible pressure through extensive marketing campaigns to buy the latest cell phone, the prettiest car, and clothes that celebrities wear. We are inundated with sales pitches through social media, news feeds, online games, television commercials, product placements in movies, and after every click on the internet. Third, we feel the need to spend more money on stuff to keep up with those around us.

> **Money Decree**
>
> Most people who say they want to be millionaires, *actually* mean they want to *spend* a million dollars, which is the exact opposite of being a millionaire.

One of the traditions I have had with my daughters since they were very young is to walk about a half mile to a coffee shop on Saturday mornings. It allows me to have some alone time with them, get some exercise, and discuss topics that might be on their minds. On one such walk, my oldest daughter (who was probably about ten at the time) spoke about a friend she had recently visited. She kept going on and on about how big and fancy their house was. It obviously made an impression on her. I asked her if their house was bigger than ours (knowing the answer because we live in a modest house for our neighborhood). She said it was much bigger. I asked her if it was nicer. She responded that it was much nicer. I asked her why she thought they had a bigger and nicer house than us. She said it was because they had more money.

From an early age in our society, we automatically assume because someone has *spent* a lot of money, they *have* a lot of money. It may very well be true, but unfortunately many times it is not.

Her assumption was that because they had a big house, they had a lot of money. This may be true. But, in reality, the only known fact is that they lived in a nice, big house. We have no idea if they owned the house without any debt, or if they had debt on the home which exceeded its value. Were they at the top of the Financial Pyramid, or living paycheck to paycheck, just with a nicer house than most?

We make assumptions and judgements every day based on what people have or what they do not. But I ask you: Why does it really matter? If someone has a bigger home or nicer car, what is the impact on you? The only true impact is that of emotion because you are coveting your neighbor's things. Coveting the things of others may cause you to buy the things that others have, which makes no sense whatsoever. What other people have is their business and has no impact on you.

Money Decree
Do not worry about what others have or buy.

Another assumption commonly made is that someone who spends a lot of money is "successful" because you believe they must have a lot of money. First, a person's success in life should never be defined by the size of their bank account, and definitely not on how much money they spend. Secondly, having a big bank account or high income certainly creates different opportunities than if you did not, but it does not guarantee success – or happiness, for that matter.

All of this is a slippery slope if we want what we don't have and try to keep up with others. Others could be spending a large portion or all their income, or worse, spending money they do not have through credit cards. If everyone else follows suit by developing those same habits, we spiral out of control toward a financial demise.

Income vs. Wealth

A key lesson here is knowing the difference between income and wealth. **Income** is the amount of money you make, most likely through a regular paycheck at your job. **Wealth** is achieved by building a substantial net worth over time.

Net worth is one way to provide a snapshot of a person's financial health and overall wealth. Net worth is calculated by taking the value of everything you own (your assets) and subtracting all your debt (your liabilities). Your assets would include things such as your house, cars, checking account, savings account, and retirement accounts. Your liabilities could be a mortgage on your home, car loans, and credit card debt. Net worth shows you how much you own versus how much you owe. Basically, the net worth calculation is adding up the total amount of equity (value) you have in everything you own. If the value of your house is currently $400,000 and you have a mortgage of $375,000, you have an equity of $25,000 ($400,000 less $375,000) for that asset.

Here is another way to think about net worth: Pretend for a moment that you sold everything you own. The amount of money you would gain from those sales is your net worth.

To keep a consistent gauge on your financial health and to measure your wealth, I recommend reviewing your net worth twice per year. This will help you track your performance over time.

Below is a simplistic example of how to calculate net worth.

Asset Values	
Home	$ 400,000
Car 1	$ 15,000
Car 2	$ 5,000
Checking account	$ 1,200
Savings account	$ 5,000
Retirement account	$ 25,000
Other possessions	$ 5,000
TOTAL ASSETS	**$ 456,200**
Liability Values	
Home mortgage	$ 375,000
Car 1 loan	$ 10,000
Car 2 loan	$ 1,500
Credit cards	$ 10,000
TOTAL LIABILITIES	**$ 396,500**
NET WORTH (Assets minus Liabilities)	**$ 59,700**

Building wealth puts people on a path to financial stability and ultimately financial independence. A high income can give you the ability to buy a lot of material things, but that does not automatically mean you are wealthy. It means you have more stuff. If you spend your entire income on an expensive house (with an expensive mortgage), a high-end car (with a high-end car loan), and lavish vacations (on your credit card), but not on savings or building equity, then you are not wealthy.

According to several studies, including the 2020 Financial Planning Survey by First National Bank of Omaha, almost half of Americans live paycheck to paycheck. That means no matter what their income, if their paychecks stopped for whatever reason, they would have a difficult time paying their bills and be catastrophic for many families.

As I have told my daughters often, one of the hardest things about having money is not spending it. I don't care if it is five dollars in your pocket or five thousand dollars in your bank account. The key to building wealth and financial success is *not* spending your entire income. That is easier said than done. However, with ongoing financial discipline by using the tips in this book, you can move in that direction.

Money is not a competition. You do not have to keep up with those around you. It is hard to see someone with nicer things than you. But who cares? It is hard not to spend cash when it is in your pocket, or to charge something on your credit card when you still have room under your credit limit. Or write a check because you still have checks left in your checkbook. The goal is to build wealth, which means you spend less than you make, and to be prudent with the money you save.

Know the difference between income and wealth, knowing that building wealth is your goal.

Chapter 6

Treat Your Money with Respect

Imagine you go for a walk in your neighborhood and you find a twenty-dollar bill. Because you're an outstanding citizen, I assume you will first look around to see if there is someone nearby who might have dropped it. If there's not, then you will pick it up and put it in your pocket. How do you feel? Does it make you feel happy and fortunate that you just received $20? Will you tell others about your good fortune?

Now, I want to turn this around and think about spending $20. How many times have you spent $20 on something you didn't need? How many times have you overpaid for a meal by $20 or more? How many times have you paid for a product or service that you could have gotten for $20 less somewhere else? I know what you're thinking, "It's only $20!" Yet, if you found $20 on the ground, it makes you happy; so saving or not spending $20 should make you feel the same way.

Buying something just because it is "only $20" is not a good reason to spend $20. With that type of habit, eventually "only $20" will turn into "only $50." Then into "only $100." How would you feel about finding $100 on the ground in front of you? You would be so ecstatic that you would tell that story to the next few people you saw and probably post it to your social media feed.

I'm not saying you shouldn't spend the money. I'm saying you should justify it before you do. Is the purchase for something you need or want? Is it something you planned for or a spontaneous purchase? Can you get the exact same or similar product or service somewhere else for a lesser price?

I know people who will only buy name brand items, whether it be clothes or cars. They are willing to pay more for certain products because of the name or brand of the manufacturer. I get it. For some products, a name is equivalent to quality and therefore justifies the increased price tag. However, in some cases the increased quality is a perception instead of reality.

Knowledge Drop

In 1914 the United States printed money in denominations ranging from $1 to $10,000. In 1969 bills greater than $100 were retired due to declining demand. Having a $10,000 bill in your wallet is just showing off.

Just before I graduated from college, I interviewed for a job with a large name brand manufacturer who made numerous food products. While touring their facility, I walked through the packaging area for oatmeal. There was a large continuous tray filled to the brim with oatmeal moving down the production line. It was dry oatmeal, but it smelled fantastic. After I swallowed my hunger, I watched as the line split into two equal trays where half of the oatmeal went to one side of the room and the other half went to the other side. Both trays then entered their respective packaging machine where oatmeal was poured into containers that would eventually end up on grocery store shelves.

I stood between the two packaging machines trying to figure out how they differed from each other. One machine had packaging with the manufacturer's name brand logo and color scheme. The other machine used packaging from a regional grocery store chain. Exact same product, two different packages, and I am sure two different sales prices. The next time you are in the grocery store, look at the name brand versus the generic brand. Do they have different quality or just different packages? Is it really worth the increased price?

> **Money Decree**
>
> Just because a product or service is more expensive, does not guarantee it is better.

Similar scenarios take place with cars. Acura is owned by Honda so they both have similar parts and manufacturing, but Acura has the luxury brand and higher price tag. The same is true for Toyota and Lexus. Do they have different quality that justifies the increased pricing?

Consumer Reports created a list of automotive brands ranked by reliability in 2020. On that list, Lexus was first out of thirty brands and Toyota third; Honda was twelfth, and Acura number twenty-eight. Of name brands and perceived high-quality luxury vehicles, BMW was number seventeen and Mercedes-Benz twenty-one. A little insight here – "luxury car" sometimes means they have cool features to help justify the price. However, the more complicated features a car has, the greater opportunity there is for the features to break, which impacts reliability.

Money is a resource that is hard to come by and should be treated as such. Treat it with respect and don't ever justify pissing it away on something you don't need by saying it is "*only* X amount of money." When you begin to justify spending your money this way, it becomes a hard habit to break.

When I was in my mid-twenties and early in my business career, I was working for a trucking company that had sales revenue exceeding $1 billion per year. One day I spoke with my boss about an expenditure the company needed to make. He discussed his decision-making around the purchase and he said to me, "The cost is only $32,000. I know that doesn't sound like much." My mouth dropped and I immediately told him I disagreed; I certainly did think that sounded like a lot of money. Considering my salary at the time was only slightly above $32,000, my perspective was much different than his. He was so used to dealing with large numbers, that $32,000 seemed insignificant to him. That is a bad trap to fall into. No matter how you look at it, $32,000 is a lot of money and should be treated as such.

During an accounting class I took in college, the professor expounded upon a concept about how to determine whether an expense was "material" between two different companies. Company A had revenue of $1 million and Company B had revenue of $500 million. His argument was that from an accounting perspective, $100,000 was immaterial to Company B because it was such a small percentage of their overall revenue. What a ridiculous concept. One hundred thousand dollars should be treated with respect because it is significant no matter how much money you have or make.

Money Decree
Money is not an infinite resource. Treat it with respect.

As your father (or mother) told you, money does not grow on trees. Money is not an infinite resource, so the money you have should be treated with respect.

Chapter 7

Know the Purpose of Your Purchase

What is the difference between a want and a need? What is the difference between an investment versus an expenditure? These are important distinctions when it comes to how you use your money and should help you prioritize the uses of your money as you budget and spend.

Want vs. Need

Basic survival needs for humans are related to food, clothing, and shelter. You need to prioritize spending money on those basic needs. However, that does not mean you should spend unlimited money on food, clothing, and shelter. Do you need to buy the largest, most beautiful house on the block? No. Do you need to shop at the most expensive clothing store, instead of discount retailers? No. Do you need to shop at the most expensive grocery store because it has a great ambience, instead of buying the same or similar items at a cheaper store? No. A need is something you *must* have to survive. Before making those everyday purchases, you should fully understand if the purchase is a need or a want. Wants should be scrutinized and justified before making the purchase.

Within our world of ever-changing technology, we can rationalize that our needs have increased dramatically over the last couple decades. Consider all the things many of us pay for every month that we didn't have when I was a child: cell phones, data plans, Wi-Fi, laptops, tablets, cable television, satellite television, and streaming services. All these things add up to extra cost in our budgets.

These technologies have become so engrained in our society it is tough to do without them. Remember that time you ran to the store and forgot your phone? How did it make you feel? Naked and afraid? Our phones are emotional attachments. We panic when we lose them, drop them, or have dead batteries.

Money Decree
Spend with a plan and purpose in mind.

Cell phone companies have done an excellent job of entrenching cell phones in our lives, starting an at an early age. How many elementary aged kids have you seen with a cell phone? Too many. From a financial perspective, save yourself money and heartache by keeping cell phones out of the hands of your young kids. They do not need a phone at that age. By taking that advice, you have now paid for this book and have the money to buy ten more books for your family and friends. You're welcome.

We now use our cell phones as clocks, cameras, calculators, calendars, weather predictors, contacts managers, search engines, email providers, and task reminders. Oh, and to make phone calls and send text messages. And that's only on the home screen.

Beyond that we use apps for our bank accounts, ride shares, airlines, hotels, directions, meditation, and social media. And that's only on the second page.

Can you imagine living without your phone? It would be tough to do because everyone expects that you have one, including your teacher, employer, customers, friends, and the companies you do business with.

The real issue here is the cost. As a family of four, we basically pay $160 per month just for a data plan. Beyond that, we pay for new phones as soon as the current ones are obsolete and no longer supported. These things are costly, and they are now a permanent part of our expenses.

We may not need phones to survive, but we must use them to participate in our world. To help manage expenses, the goal should be to buy what you need, not necessarily what you want. You do not need the latest and greatest cell phone as soon as it hits the market. Buy an older model that will do what you need without killing your bank account. This is true with every facet of technology. You should not buy the latest and greatest – but on the other hand, do not buy the cheapest or oldest either because it may be obsolete soon and could open you up to cyber security issues. Buy technology somewhere in the middle, so you get what you need at a more reasonable cost.

Investment vs. Expenditure

As we grow older and hopefully become more established financially, we must begin focusing our financial attention on our needs and become more concerned with building wealth. An initial step in building wealth is understanding the difference between a purchase made for an investment versus for an expenditure.

Purchasing investments helps us build wealth because we are buying something today in anticipation it will grow in value. We buy an investment with a hope it will build equity (or value) over the time we own the investment. When we sell the item, we get a return on our investment by receiving more money than we paid.

Homes are generally the largest purchase you will make in your lifetime, and if done correctly, they are great investments. Using simple math, if you buy a home for $250,000 today, and ten years from now it is worth $400,000, then you have $150,000 worth of equity. Your asset (home) grew in value and helped you build an additional $150,000 in wealth.

A simple expenditure is when you buy a product or service that will provide no return on your investment over time. These products may have some value initially but will lose value over the time you own them and will not help you build wealth.

Below are a few examples of purchases that gain value over time (investments) versus lose money over time (expenditures).

GAIN VALUE	LOSE VALUE
Home / Land	Car
Savings Account	Boat
Money Market	Motorcycles
Certificate of Deposits	Clothes
Stocks	Furniture
Bonds	Televisions
Mutual Funds	Cell Phones
Retirement Accounts	
College Savings Accounts	

Those that can spend more money on investments and control their spending will build wealth and move up the Financial Pyramid toward financial independence. Purchasing investments builds wealth; everything else takes away from it.

Chapter 8

Just Because You Can Afford Something Doesn't Mean You Should Buy It

Can you afford a brand-new car? A bigger house? To pay someone to take care of your yard or swimming pool? To eat out every night? What does "afford" really mean? Simply, if you have the available cash to pay for a purchase, then you can afford the purchase. Or you can afford to get a loan and make the payments on that loan for a new house, a new car, or whatever else you want to spend the money on.

Whether or not you can afford something can be a debate because it means different things to different people. Some may say if they have more room on their credit card before they hit a limit, they can afford to buy something. Others may say if they do not have cash right now to buy something, they cannot afford it.

Either way, just because you can afford a purchase, does not necessarily mean you should make the purchase. This is why it's so important to identify your financial goals and establish a plan for making money (Part II of this book), saving money (Part III), and spending money (Part IV). If you spend all your money on everything you can "afford" before meeting your plans for saving, then saving will take a back seat to spending and it will be much harder to move up the Financial Pyramid toward your goal.

For me, I say we can "afford" something if it is part of our financial planning and budgeting, keeping in mind that saving money is a large portion of our budget.

One of the hardest things about having money is not spending it, especially on things you don't need. I see it with my kids all the time. They receive cash for chores, from their jobs, or as a gift and they immediately want to spend it on something. They want candy or clothes even though before they had the money, there was no plan to spend it on candy or clothes.

Money Decree
One of the hardest things about having money is not spending it.

As adults, we continue with the same habits. Our paychecks drop into our bank accounts and our goal becomes spending until every available dollar is gone. The key is developing your plan for that paycheck ahead of time, so it gets used properly. A portion should be used for everyday expenses and a portion for savings.

Over the years, there were a lot of things our family could "afford," but that didn't always mean we would buy them. Why? Because we wanted to build wealth and financial independence. We chose to make short-term sacrifices to achieve our long-term goals. The sacrifice was to not buy something we wanted because we did not need it.

Some attribute this to me being tight-ass or cheap, and they are probably right. But how else was I to achieve my goals, if I didn't control my spending first?

We typically spend less than we can afford so the available income can be put into various savings and retirement accounts for future use. This can be seen in a few examples in our lives:

- My wife and I currently own two vehicles that were moderately priced when we bought them. Both were purchased with loans with minimal interest and were paid off early. One is now eight years old with 90,000 miles on it and the other is twelve years old with 110,000 miles. We have chosen to not buy newer vehicles because these are working just fine, and we would rather spend money elsewhere or save it for future use.

- Our home is mid-sized and mid-priced for our community, even though we could afford a bigger and nicer home. It would be great to have more space and a bigger yard, but we choose to stay where we are because this house is just fine and gives us all the comforts we need. The house is in a great location, with great schools nearby.
- We choose not to pay anyone else to do our yard work, manage our pool, or clean our house. We can afford to have someone else do those things and it would be nice to outsource those tasks, but we continue to do them ourselves because we can, and we would rather spend that money elsewhere (or not spend it at all). Doing yard work can be hard and time consuming (and not fun in the Arizona summer heat), but it helps me stay in shape.

If you spend every single dollar you make, you will never get ahead and move towards being comfortable financially. Set your goals and budget to work toward financial stability and independence.

Now that you understand the underlying concepts about money, we move into the real-world tips and concepts to help you get where you want to go – up the Financial Pyramid.

PART II:

MAKING MONEY

Chapter 9

A Job Is About More Than Pay

I hope throughout your life when you are looking for a job, you have an endless supply of options to choose from. Unfortunately, many times that will not be the case. In a thriving economy, job opportunities are easier to find, and you can take your time to evaluate each option for the right choice. Other times, when the economy may not be doing as well, you get what you get, and you don't throw a fit.

The best time to find another job is when you are currently employed. This gives you the opportunity to make a choice with less pressure because you are already receiving a paycheck. In those times where you are unemployed, you are more anxious about taking the first job opportunity you find because being unemployed is nerve-wracking and emotional.

No matter the situation, be sure that when you are talking about a job with a prospective employer, look at the entire package they have to offer. Even though you go to work for money, there are many other factors to consider beyond your pay rate that have an equal impact on your overall financial situation. This means you need to scrutinize potential jobs to ensure you have full knowledge about what the company has to offer.

Looking beyond the pay rate, other factors used to evaluate a company's job offer to you can be broken into two parts: benefits and work environment.

Benefits

A benefit is something offered by a company in addition to your regular pay. Some benefits come with an additional cost and others are offered at no additional cost to you. Companies use benefits to remain competitive in the job market, to attract talented people to their company, and to provide support to their current employees so they continue working at the company for a long time.

Most, but not all, benefits are offered to full-time employees, meaning you must work at least 40 hours per week to be eligible. However, every business is different, so ask questions and get information about all the benefits offered and available to you in the job.

Along with the benefit details, make sure you understand the cost tied to each benefit. You don't want to take a job because you are enamored by the pay and benefits only to find the benefits are so expensive, they eat up your entire paycheck. When you are offered a job, your pay and a few benefits (such as vacation) can be negotiable, but very rarely are the costs of benefits negotiable. Expect to pay the listed costs and expect them to increase in price each year.

Let's look at a list of possible benefits a company could offer its employees. This list shows common benefits many companies offer, but every company is different, so it is important to ask and get your comprehensive benefits list in writing.

- *Health insurance* – Insurance to pay for doctor's visits, hospital visits, emergency care, and medications for you and your family.
- *Dental insurance* – Insurance to pay for visits to the dentist or dental emergencies.

- *Vision insurance* – Insurance to pay for visits to the eye doctor along with glasses and contacts.
- *Healthcare spending or reimbursement accounts (HSA, HRA)* – These accounts allow you to put pre-tax money into an account to spend on future medical expenses. We will discuss pre-tax deductions in the next chapter.
- *401k retirement plan* – This allows you to take pre-tax dollars and invest it for retirement.
- *401k matching* – Many employers will contribute money to your 401k or match a certain amount of money you invest as a benefit of working for them. This is free money given to you so you can use it for retirement.
- *Life insurance* – Insurance that is paid to a loved one in case you die. Many companies will provide a life insurance policy at no additional cost to you, along with an opportunity to increase the value of the policy for an additional cost.
- *Short-term disability* – Insurance paid over a very short period (days or a few weeks) in case you cannot work for various reasons.
- *Long-term disability* – Insurance paid over a longer period (weeks or months) in case you cannot work for various reasons.
- *Paid time off (PTO), vacation and/or sick days* – Pay for days when you are not at work while on vacation, if you are sick, or need time off for personal reasons.
- *College tuition reimbursement* – Payment or reimbursement of college tuition expenses to an employee under certain guidelines.
- *Profit sharing, bonus programs, or stock purchase programs* – Companies may offer a percentage of their profits to their employees as an incentive. This can be done in various ways, including through your paycheck or in the form of ownership in the company.
- *Discounts on products sold by the company* – Many times employees have the option of buying the company products at drastically reduced rates.

- *Wellness programs* – To motivate employees to stay healthy, companies may offer discounts to gyms, training on healthy habits, and/or ways to stop smoking.

When you are fortunate enough to get a job offer from a company, make sure you get it in writing. No matter the complexity of a job offer, it is important to have them detailed on paper for a couple of reasons. First, getting a job offer is very exciting. Everyone wants to be wanted, and it is exciting when a company says they want *you* to come work for them. Your heart beats faster and your mind races, wondering what you will wear on your first day on the job. During all that excitement, some details can be lost or missed. Get all the details in writing so you can review the offer when your heart rate goes back to normal, and your excitement subsides.

Secondly, a written document ensures everyone is crystal clear about what the offer is and there is no confusion about any of those details. I learned this lesson the hard way.

> **Knowledge Drop**
>
> In 1938 the Fair Labor Standards Act was passed, creating the first minimum wage standards at 25 cents per hour.

Several years ago, a company offered a job to me over the phone, which I accepted. The job was with a small company in a different state, so we were required to relocate. The job offer was not overly complicated, but there were a few details which were important. My wife and I were excited about moving to a new city and taking advantage of this job opportunity. We moved, got settled, and I started work. But when I got my first paycheck, my rate of pay was different than my expectation. I immediately brought it up to my supervisor and he was adamant my pay was correct and it was the exact same number he provided me over the phone during the negotiation. I was certain he was wrong.

I have no idea who was in the right, but because we did not get it in writing, I had no recourse. From that day forward, all my job offers were in writing, whether they were offers given to me or if I were giving them to prospective employees.

At a minimum, the job offer should include the following details:

- Position, along with a job description
- Name of direct supervisor
- Start date
- Status (full-time vs. part-time, hourly vs. salaried)
- Basic work schedule
- Rate of pay
- Pay schedule (when you get paid and how often)
- Benefits offered (ideally with a cost schedule)
- Signatures of the employer and you

Now let's dig further in how to evaluate a job offer by reviewing a simple scenario. We'll pretend you currently have a job, but you were just offered a new job with a different company.

You should grab a piece of paper and make a comparison list of the pay and benefits for each job to help you decide. Your list could look something like the one shown below. For simplicity reasons, we won't discuss taxes taken out of your check here so our math is easier.

	CURRENT JOB	NEW JOB
Pay	$500 per week	$600 per week
Health insurance	$50 per week	$100 per week
Dental insurance	$0 per week	$15 per week
Vision insurance	$0 per week	$10 per week
401k matching	5%	No 401k plan
Paid time off (PTO)	2 weeks per year	1 week per year
College Tuition Reimbursement	Yes, if you get a B grade or better	No college tuition reimbursement

Which one would you choose? If you focus on the pay only, you will think it was a no-brainer – you get a pay increase of $100 per week. But when you dig deeper, that is not the real story.

Your current job pays you $500 per week minus $50 per week for health insurance, making your pay $450 per week.

The new job pays you $600 per week, but the costs for health, dental, and vision insurance are $125 per week, leaving you $475.

The bottom line is you would get a $25 per week increase in pay, but you no longer have a retirement plan, the retirement plan matching, or college reimbursement, plus you lost half your vacation. Is the extra $25 per week worth it? Since you are reading a book about personal finance and how you should save more money to move up the Financial Pyramid, let's assume the answer is *no*!

A 401k retirement plan is a primary method to increase retirement savings, and to lose that benefit (along with the 5 percent company matching) would be a poor financial decision. The new job also removes an opportunity to further your education without any cost to you. And you need vacation time, so do not give up a week of paid time off over $25.

Different benefits should have different priorities depending on your age and needs at the time. As you get older and build a family, many of these benefits become more important to ensure your entire family is cared for. However, when you are on your own and starting with your first real job it is important that at a minimum you get health insurance and a retirement plan. You must protect yourself in case you get sick, and you should start diverting money into your retirement account as soon as you possibly can – even if it is only ten dollars a week.

Work Environment

The second factor you should consider when evaluating a job offer is the work environment.

Over my professional business career, I have done hundreds of job interviews with prospective employees. One of my common questions was, "What was the best job you ever had and why?" Ninety-nine times out of a hundred, a person will tell me the reason they liked a specific job was because of the work environment, which included the people they worked with and their supervisor. They did not say it was because of the money. The money is (and should be) important. But if you enjoy your job because of the environment, positive things will happen.

Here is a list of factors you should consider when evaluating a job:

- How many hours will you be working? Know whether it is part time or full time, and if there are specific hours of the day you will be working. Will this be enough hours to meet your budget requirements for income or is it too many hours that conflict with other parts of your life, such as your family? If you are an hourly employee, is there an opportunity to earn overtime and the higher pay associated with it?
- Who is your supervisor, and do you feel like you would get along with them?
- Where will you be working within the company? Is it outside with no air conditioning or a luxurious corner office looking at the beautiful skyline?
- Are there opportunities for advancement with the company? If you work hard and excel in your current job, is there an opportunity to move up?
- Is there a training program for new employees? Does the company support continuing education and professional development? If so, how?
- How long has the company been in business? Many brand-new businesses struggle for the first few years, so it is important to know how long they have been around. This does not mean you should not work for a brand-new company, only that you should know there is a risk and potential sacrifice in doing so.
- How large is the company? Do you want to be a small fish in a big pond where you are one of the hundreds or thousands of employees? This may be a more stable environment with more advancement opportunities, but it could also be a

scenario where it is harder to be recognized for your efforts because of the company's size. Or would you rather be a big fish in a small pond where you would be required to wear multiple hats in a small business?

- How is the commute or is there an opportunity to work remotely? Consider the distance from your home to the job and what traffic and/or weather will be like during various times of the day throughout the year. A bad commute can be tolerated for a short period of time, but driving in bumper to bumper traffic daily can grind on you. Driving long distances during the winter months can be challenging in many locations. Consider how you would feel driving in snowy, icy, or rainy conditions. I have had extremes when it comes to commuting. I had a 45-mile commute on an interstate that was only a real problem when it rained (which was more days than not). I have also had a 13-mile commute that could take 45 minutes to an hour due to traffic. I do not miss either one.

Be sure to recognize which factors are important to you so you can discuss them with your prospective employer or observe them while participating in the interview process.

So, what does all this have to do with your money? If you do not like the work environment of your job, you will not be happy with the company, and it is possible the company will not be happy with you. Which may cause you to look for another job at this point.

Sometimes moving from one job to another is important for various reasons, but I caution you not to be a job hopper. Unless you are desperate for income, only take a job if you intend on staying there at least three years or more. If you have several jobs where you worked for only a short period of time, prospective employers may not consider you over other candidates with a more stable work history. Hiring costs companies a lot of money and they do not want to hire and train someone that will leave shortly thereafter, because then they have to start all over again. Eventually, this will catch up with you and it will impact your earning potential.

Additionally, if you are happy and passionate about your job, you are more likely to excel and be recognized for advancement opportunities. This can gain you more money through pay raises, additional benefits, or increased responsibilities and promotions.

All of us have interacted with an employee in a business who obviously hates their job. It is not a pleasant experience as a customer, and it certainly does not reflect well on the business or the employee.

Chapter 10

A Lot of People Take Money Out of Your Check

Remember the "Friends" episode when Rachel got her first paycheck from her first real job in the coffee shop? She is so happy and excited as she holds up the envelope containing her paycheck. As she opens it, she exclaims to her friends, "I earned this! I wiped tables for it, I steamed milk for it, and it was totally ... not worth it." She stares at her check with a bewildered look. "Who is FICA and why is he getting all my money?"

As teenagers, you grow up with people giving you cash for doing work such as babysitting, dog watching, or yard work. But then you get to the adulting world where paychecks are real – and taxable.

As a part of living in the United States and whatever state you live in, you must pay taxes to our federal, state, and local governments to support a myriad of things such as schools, roads, military defense, health programs, and interest on the country's national debt (because the government does not do well with money). The amount of tax you owe our government will depend on the amount of your taxable income. Each year you must file federal and state tax returns by April 15, showing the amount of income you had for the previous year.

In your earlier adult years, most, if not all, of your taxable income will come from your paychecks. As you get older and build wealth, you may receive income from other sources, including stock market investments or various types of savings accounts.

Each year, by February 1, every company you worked for as an employee during the previous year will send you a document called a W2. This document is required so you can fill out your tax returns and file them by the April 15 deadline. The W2 will provide several pieces of information including the amount your employer paid you during the year. An example of what a W2 looks like is below.

22222	a Employee's social security number 123-45-6789	OMB No. 1545-0008	
b Employer identification number (EIN) 11-2233444		1 Wages, tips, other compensation $47,000.00	2 Federal income tax withheld $4,700.00
c Employer's name, address, and ZIP code Big Employer 123 Easy Street Washington, DC 12345		3 Social security wages $50,000.00	4 Social security tax withheld $3,100.00
		5 Medicare wages and tips $50,000.00	6 Medicare tax withheld $725.00
		7 Social security tips	8 Allocated tips
d Control number		9	10 Dependent care benefits
e Employee's first name and initial	Last name Suff.	11 Nonqualified plans	12a
Ima B. Taxpayer 456 Main Street Philadelphia, PA 12345		13 Statutory employee / Retirement plan / Third-party sick pay	12b
		14 Other	12c
f Employee's address and ZIP code			12d

15 State	Employer's state ID number	16 State wages, tips, etc.	17 State income tax	18 Local wages, tips, etc.	19 Local income tax	20 Locality name
PA	55-222222222	$50,000.00	$1,535.00	$50,000.00	$800.00	TGP

Form **W-2** Wage and Tax Statement 2020

Department of the Treasury—Internal Revenue Service

Copy 1—For State, City, or Local Tax Department

The process of completing tax returns will calculate your total taxable income and how much tax you owe on that income. But instead of you just writing a check one time per year for the taxes you owe, your employer will take taxes out of each paycheck and pay them on your behalf to help offset your annual tax bill. It is like a payment plan to the government.

Because of complicated tax laws and paid hours that can fluctuate from paycheck to paycheck, it may be difficult to know the exact dollar of tax you owe over a year's time. To ensure you have paid the correct amount, you fill out tax forms detailing the amount of your income and the amount withheld from your paychecks for federal and state taxes. All the required payroll information will be found on your W2, including how much you made in gross income, and how much tax you have already paid to both the federal and state government through your regular paychecks.

Knowledge Drop

The W-2 Form was established by the Current Tax Payment Act of 1943 and were first published in 1944.

The primary purpose of the tax returns is to "shore up" your annual tax number. Once you completely fill out the tax return, it will show how much tax you owe versus how much you already paid. Then you must take care of the difference. If you owe $1,000 in tax, but you only paid $900 through your paychecks, you need to write the government a check for $100. If you owe $1,000 in tax and you paid $1,100 in tax through your paychecks, you will get a $100 refund from the government.

Most people get very excited when they get a refund, and not so much when they must pay additional funds at the end of the year. In reality, it should be the other way around.

If you are getting a refund, that means you paid more money to the government than what you needed to, and you basically just gave them a free loan. They keep your money, but they do not pay you any interest in return. They just keep it and use it however they want. Do not use the government as your savings account for money by intentionally overpaying them each year just so you get a refund. There are better ways to use your money.

Knowledge Drop

The IRS processed more than 240.2 million Federal tax returns and supplemental documents in fiscal year 2020.

In theory, the ideal situation is that you pay exactly what you owe in taxes through your paychecks and your tax return shows no refund or payment required. Since that is nearly impossible due to fluctuating income and complicated tax laws, ideally you should get to know your tax situation so well that every year you owe a little bit of money to the government.

No time in your life would you ever want to pay someone *more* money than you owe them. Could you imagine going to a grocery store to buy twenty dollars' worth of items, but then giving them thirty dollars and saying, "Just hang on to it for next time"? I know that sounds ridiculous, but that is exactly what you are doing if you knowingly pay more to the government so you can always get a refund each year.

Even though your tax will be calculated based on your taxable income for the year, you can make the amount of taxes removed from your paycheck be anything you want. Employees fill out a form called a W4 (see an example shown) to detail the amount of tax they want removed from each paycheck. The IRS provides a tax estimator which will help you determine your approximate tax over the year. The tax estimator can be found at https://apps.irs.gov/app/tax-withholding-estimator. This calculator will give you a good starting

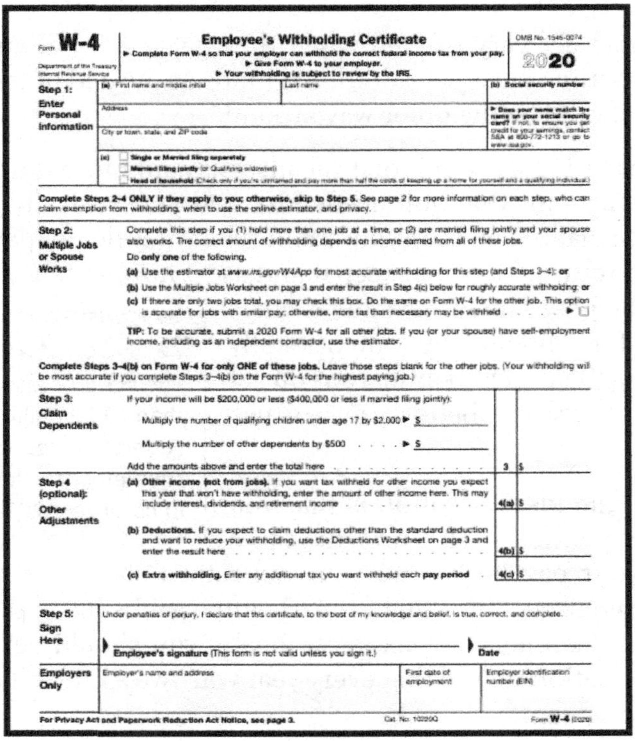

Form **W-4**
Department of the Treasury
Internal Revenue Service

Employee's Withholding Certificate
▶ Complete Form W-4 so that your employer can withhold the correct federal income tax from your pay.
▶ Give Form W-4 to your employer.
▶ Your withholding is subject to review by the IRS.

OMB No. 1545-0074
2020

Step 1: Enter Personal Information
(a) First name and middle initial | Last name | (b) Social security number
Address
City or town, state, and ZIP code
▶ **Does your name match the name on your social security card?** If not, to ensure you get credit for your earnings, contact SSA at 800-772-1213 or go to www.ssa.gov.
(c) ☐ **Single or Married filing separately**
☐ **Married filing jointly** (or Qualifying widow(er))
☐ **Head of household** (Check only if you're unmarried and pay more than half the costs of keeping up a home for yourself and a qualifying individual.)

Complete Steps 2–4 ONLY if they apply to you; otherwise, skip to Step 5. See page 2 for more information on each step, who can claim exemption from withholding, when to use the online estimator, and privacy.

Step 2: Multiple Jobs or Spouse Works
Complete this step if you (1) hold more than one job at a time, or (2) are married filing jointly and your spouse also works. The correct amount of withholding depends on income earned from all of these jobs.
Do **only one** of the following.
(a) Use the estimator at *www.irs.gov/W4App* for most accurate withholding for this step (and Steps 3–4); **or**
(b) Use the Multiple Jobs Worksheet on page 3 and enter the result in Step 4(c) below for roughly accurate withholding; **or**
(c) If there are only two jobs total, you may check this box. Do the same on Form W-4 for the other job. This option is accurate for jobs with similar pay; otherwise, more tax than necessary may be withheld . . . . . . ▶ ☐
TIP: To be accurate, submit a 2020 Form W-4 for all other jobs. If you (or your spouse) have self-employment income, including as an independent contractor, use the estimator.

Complete Steps 3–4(b) on Form W-4 for only ONE of these jobs. Leave those steps blank for the other jobs. (Your withholding will be most accurate if you complete Steps 3–4(b) on the Form W-4 for the highest paying job.)

Step 3: Claim Dependents
If your income will be $200,000 or less ($400,000 or less if married filing jointly):
Multiply the number of qualifying children under age 17 by $2,000 ▶ $
Multiply the number of other dependents by $500 . . . . ▶ $
Add the amounts above and enter the total here . . . . 3 $

Step 4 (optional): Other Adjustments
(a) Other income (not from jobs). If you want tax withheld for other income you expect this year that won't have withholding, enter the amount of other income here. This may include interest, dividends, and retirement income . . . . 4(a) $
(b) Deductions. If you expect to claim deductions other than the standard deduction and want to reduce your withholding, use the Deductions Worksheet on page 3 and enter the result here . . . . 4(b) $
(c) Extra withholding. Enter any additional tax you want withheld each **pay period** . 4(c) $

Step 5: Sign Here
Under penalties of perjury, I declare that this certificate, to the best of my knowledge and belief, is true, correct, and complete.
▶ **Employee's signature** (This form is not valid unless you sign it.) ▶ **Date**

Employers Only
Employer's name and address | First date of employment | Employer identification number (EIN)

For Privacy Act and Paperwork Reduction Act Notice, see page 3. Cat. No. 10220Q Form **W-4** (2020)

point for how much tax to take out of your check, but each year you can adjust the amount of money you want withheld based on the previous year's tax return.

If you get a refund, you can reduce the withholding to take less money out of your check. If you have a large tax bill, you can increase the withholding to take more money out of your check. You can withhold any amount you want, but just understand your tax return will determine the difference, so get as close as you can. A huge refund or huge tax bill are both bad for different reasons. A refund was a free loan to your government, and on the other hand, nobody wants a large, unexpected bill. Especially if that bill is payable to the government.

Knowledge Drop

According to IRS data, about three in four Americans receive a tax refund each year and the average amount returned with those refunds is around $3,000.

For the most part, the more money you make, the more tax you will owe. However, there are certain legal strategies to manage the amount of your tax. One strategy is to lower the amount of taxable income on your paychecks. You can do this by designating specific deductions from your paycheck on a pre-tax basis. That means you make certain deductions from your income before the federal, state, and local taxes are calculated. This lowers your income that is taxable. There are several deductions which can be taken out pre-tax, including insurance premiums for health, dental, and vision, health savings accounts, and retirement plan deductions. In most cases, these are automatically designated as pre-tax deductions when you sign up for these specific programs with your employer.

See the chart on the next page for a simple example of how pre-tax deductions work and how they can benefit you. Understand that this is a pretend example to show you the important impact of pre-tax deductions. In reality, the types of deductions shown in the example are typically pre-tax deductions automatically.

In this example, I have shown two scenarios of paychecks detailed side by side. The first column shows the deductions taken out *post-*

tax, meaning your taxes are calculated on your gross pay, and your deductions are then subtracted.

The second column shows the deductions taken out *pre-tax*, meaning they are subtracted from your gross pay before the tax is calculated.

	Post-Tax Deductions	Pre-tax Deductions
Gross Pay	$500.00	$500.00
Health insurance deduction	$50.00	$50.00
Dental insurance deduction	$10.00	$10.00
Vision insurance deduction	$5.00	$5.00
401k deduction	$20.00	$20.00
Taxable Income	$500.00	$415.00
Tax (25% of Taxable Income)	$125.00	$103.75
Paycheck Amount	$290.00	$311.25

In both scenarios, your gross pay is $500, and you have various deductions for insurance and a retirement plan that reduce your paycheck amount. In this example, your tax is 25 percent of your taxable income.

The two scenarios detail how pre-tax deductions change the amount of your taxable income, which lowers your tax, and ultimately increases your take home pay.

The first column that says "Post-Tax Deductions" is an example of your paycheck if you took the insurance and retirement deductions after your tax was calculated. In this scenario, your taxable income is $500 which causes your tax to be $125 ($500 x 25%). After all the deductions are made this brings your take home pay to $290.

In the second scenario, we show insurance and retirement deductions to come out pre-tax. In this case, your taxable income is $415 instead of $500 because we removed the deductions first. The tax becomes $103.75 ($415 x 25%) and your take home pay is $311.25.

By making your deductions pre-tax, your tax went down from $125.00 to $103.75 and your take home pay went up to $311.25 instead of $290.00.

This is a win, win – lower taxes and higher take home pay.

Now, let's go over several of the tax deductions that will come out of your paycheck. They include:

- *FICA:* The United States federal payroll tax. It stands for the Federal Insurance Contributions Act. The amount deducted is based on your specific tax situation. The tax is a percentage of your taxable income. The amount of your deduction is determined by how you filled out the federal W4 form.
- *State Tax:* This is the state payroll tax for whichever state you live in. The amount deducted is based on your specific tax situation. The tax is a percentage of your taxable income. The amount of your deduction is determined by how you filled out the state W4 form.
- *Medicare:* This is an insurance program administered by the government. You pay money into the program, and you will be able to withdraw money from the program as soon as you meet an eligibility requirement, such as your age. The tax is a fixed percentage of your taxable income.
- *Social Security:* This is another insurance program administered by the government. You pay money into the program, and you will be able to withdraw money from the

program as soon as you meet eligibility requirements, such as your age. This program is thought of by many as a *retirement plan,* but that was not the purpose of the program, nor should you depend on it for all your retirement income. The tax is a fixed percentage of your taxable income.

Chapter 11

Do Not Expect Promotions and Raises – Earn Them

I have been in business for over 25 years, including owning a company with 140 awesome employees. Over my career, I have worked with a myriad of employees. Some were excellent people who were very passionate about their work, and others not so much. Those who excel and thrive within companies are those who are aligned with the goals of the organization and help the company become better for its customers and other employees. They work hard with a positive attitude.

Do not get caught up in a common misconception that a company "owes" you something just because you are a nice person, or because you have worked at the business longer than anyone else. Those things are important, but the business was established to sell their products and services to customers for a profit. They are legally, morally, and ethically obligated to offer a safe working environment, treat you with respect, and pay you a competitive wage. You are morally and ethically obligated to put forth your best effort to meet the required responsibilities of the job. Beyond that, there are no guarantees in life.

More often than not, the largest increases in your income happen by taking on jobs with more responsibility. You become a greater asset to the company because you are willing and able to take on these greater responsibilities successfully, and the company rewards you with higher paychecks.

With that said, my advice for you is to earn promotions and raises, not expect them. Below are a few guidelines that can make it more likely for you to earn promotions and raises. If you do not follow these rules and expect promotions and raises to be handed to you, then you will be disappointed. Put yourself in a position where you are an asset to the company and good things will follow.

Be Educated

A proper education is an investment. Like any investment, if it is used correctly, then you will see a return on that investment. Get an education after high school that includes a four-year college degree, community college degree, or a vocational school. Identify a field you are interested in and start learning so you can be an asset to any company hiring you.

Never Stop Learning

Getting a job is only a small part of the overall process. Learning more details about the job and the company you work for is critical to moving up within the organization. Get a handle on your current job and become an expert. Then, start spending a little bit of time learning about what other people do within the company and increase your skill set. This process will help prepare you for the next step within the company. If the company offers tuition reimbursement or opportunities to attend seminars or classes to learn new skills or improve the ones you already have, take advantage of it. In a situation like that, you not only get a free education, but you also gain new or improved skills and an opportunity to earn more money.

Be Trustworthy

Ensure that whatever responsibilities you are given, you do them to the best of your ability. Be trusted with the responsibilities you are given, and you will receive more. Exceed expectations whenever you can.

My first job out of college was with a large trucking company. They hired me into their management training program at the corporate office where we learned about different facets of the company before being placed somewhere within the organization. Even though this was not broadcasted, you were looked at by the management team as you moved through the organization and then the management team would select which trainees to hire within their respective departments.

During a two- or three-week period during the training, I was assigned to the flatbed division within the company. Flatbeds are the trailers without sides. They haul specialized equipment or products that need to be unloaded from the sides or top. The division was small and unique compared to the rest of the company, which was known for its more traditional box trailers.

One day, I very briefly met the president of the division and he told me that it would be great if someone would put together an operating manual for them to use for future reference. He knew the division was unique and he wanted to identify ways to explain how they were different from the rest of the company, but also establish common operating practices for the division. He mentioned it to me once, with little or no detail, and little expectation. In fact, I would not even classify it as an assignment he gave me. He was just thinking out loud.

Over the next couple weeks, I worked my butt off on completing that operating manual. I worked on it at home after the regular workday was done, or during any free moment I found. Hell, I do not even know if he remembered the conversation, but the look on his face when I gave him the manual said it all. He was thrilled because I exceeded expectations. Soon after, he offered me a job. I spent the next five years in his division, and I moved up in the organization quickly. He knew he could trust me with the remedial tasks as well as the big ones. That paid off big for both of us. I cannot think of a better way to start my professional career and I would not have changed it for the world.

My last point about being trustworthy seems simple, yet many people struggle with the concept. Show up for work on time and on every scheduled workday. Your supervisor and your peers depend on you to be there for work, and if you do not show up someone else has to take up the slack. However, if you are sick, then stay home. It is incredibly important to take care of your health and there is no point in getting others in the office sick along with you.

Be Ethical

The biggest thing you build in your career or personal life is the reputation of your name. Act appropriately so whenever anyone mentions your name, they only think good things. Do not be a name that is associated with shady business practices, playing office politics, or bad-mouthing others. It will always come back to haunt you.

Be a Great Teammate

You can be the smartest person in the room and have the greatest gifts known to man – but none of that means anything if you cannot work with (and for) other people. If you are a likeable person, you will go further in your career – and in life – than if you are not. Be good to your fellow employees, bosses, subordinates, customers, and vendors. You never know how your daily interactions with others will impact your career down the line.

Work Really Hard

Be the employee that does everything they are told and a whole lot more. There is always something to do in a business. You can help wipe off tables, empty the garbage, clean up the bathrooms, stock the shelves, help customers, etc. Never stand around idly chitchatting with other employees or texting on your phone. If you have completed a task assigned, find another one.

Come in early and stay late. Take extra work when asked. Take on extra responsibility when offered, even if it does not provide additional pay. Communicate new ideas to help improve customer service or the work environment. Be part of a solution to make the company better.

With that said, I think it is also important to understand some rules around this advice. First, you need to be paid for work you complete. If you are an employee that is paid by the hour and asked to complete work while not being paid – that is not ok. In fact, it is very illegal. If you are a salaried employee just know that you may be asked to perform work outside of regular business hours. This is a common business practice that should be expected. Secondly, recognize there should be a work/life balance. Working too much can cause you to mentally wear down or put a strain on your relationships. It is important to work hard, but not to the detriment of your important relationships or mental health.

Ask for More Responsibility

If you think you are ready for more responsibility, ask for it. When you get to a point that you have mastered your current job, then sit down and talk with your supervisor. Let them know you want to help them and the company by learning new jobs and responsibilities or discuss other opportunities where they feel you could be a good fit. Never demand or dictate what you think *your* needs are. Approach it from the needs of the company and supervisor by asking how you can help and develop your talents for the betterment of the organization.

Have on hand those skills you have gained while working with the organization and remind your supervisor about your commitments to come early, stay late, and help out the company when needed.

Good organizations will work with you on action plans that you can develop before moving to the next level. These may include taking classes or working to improve on things such as organizational skills, typing, or public speaking.

Be Loyal

When you take a job offer from a company, that comes with responsibility. Do the jobs they ask, in the best way you possibly can. In return, you get paid. Intend on spending time with that company and living up to your obligations.

The company spent time finding you, interviewing you, and training you. You are an investment, so act like it. If you give them a return on their investment, you will receive dividends through more opportunities and higher pay. Sometimes you must stick it out and be patient for those things to happen.

Focus on a goal of staying with a company for at least three years or more. When you do decide to leave, always provide a two-week notice at a minimum.

No matter how much you hate your job and your boss, always give a notice that you are leaving the company. The notice should be in writing and professionally written. More time than not, your termination notice should be very short and sweet - "This will serve as notice that I will terminate my employment on July 25, 2022. Please let me know how I can help with this transition. I appreciate the opportunity to work for the company." Then you sign and date the document.

There are a few exceptions to this rule that could include an unsafe working environment, illegal activities within the organization, or unethical behavior such as harassment. If you have any of these issues, report them immediately and exit the company rapidly if they are not remedied in a timely manner.

Sometimes You Must Leave to Advance

If you have done everything right, but there are no opportunities for advancement, or you are ready for more responsibility and bigger challenges that do not exist, then leave. Always leave on good terms. Provide a notice of termination and do not bad mouth the company or its employees to anyone before, during, or after you leave the company. More times than not, burning a bridge may make you feel better in the moment, but it serves no purpose and may hurt you down the road.

I remember reading a story about a flight attendant who decided to quit his job while the plane he was working on was sitting on an active taxiway. He opened the main door, inflated the emergency slide, and slid down. It was a pretty funny story and everyone fantasizes about quitting their job in a unique and satisfying way, but do you think he ever got another job in the airline industry again? Never burn a bridge. Or inflate an airplane slide on a runway.

However, if you work for a company that is unethical with employees, customers, or vendors, or doing something illegal – get out as soon as you can. There is a significant difference between a poorly run company and one that is doing something intentionally wrong. In the next chapter, we will discuss more about the obligations of a company to you and how that should impact when you leave a job.

Money Decree
Earn job promotions and raises, do not just expect them.

After college, I worked at my first company for five and a half years. I was at the top of the management organizational chart unless I wanted to move to the corporate offices in a different part of the United States, which was not appealing to me. I felt like I was getting a little bored and needed a new challenge, along with more responsibility (and money). The only way to achieve those things was to look elsewhere. I began searching for another job and ended up moving to a competitor.

I vividly remember the conversation with my supervisor (which was that same division president I wrote about earlier) when I gave my resignation notice. He took a deep breath and said, "Who got you?" I responded with the name of the competitor. I told him I would give him two weeks' notice or more if he needed me to stay longer. He said, "Usually when one of my employees leaves to go to a competitor, we walk them out the door immediately. But I trust you too damn much. Two weeks will be fine." That is the way to leave a job in good standing.

Chapter 12

All Jobs (and Companies) Are Not Created Equal

Over your career, you will have jobs that are really good, some that are really bad, and a few just because you really need a job. Treat all of them with the same vigor, because every one of them is a learning experience and provides you money.

I have learned just as much from bad companies I have worked for than I have from the good ones. The same goes for supervisors. Unfortunately, most times bad experiences provide you a better lesson. Bad experiences can be more memorable because of the mark they leave on your brain. Even when you are working a part time job over the summer during your teenage years – learn all the good and all the bad things about being in the workforce. All those lessons will pay dividends down the road.

As I reflect on my career, a diverse number of experiences (both good and bad) over the years allowed me to have the knowledge and experience to eventually become the CEO of a struggling company and lead it to success. Every single job will teach you something, if you pay attention. All that knowledge will help you become a better person, grow in your career, and help you make more money over your lifetime. Opportunities are only opportunities if you recognize them and take advantage of them. Recognizing them in every job you have will help you grow as a person. Sometimes it is tough to find those opportunities, particularly in bad jobs, but they always exist. Find them so you can grow, learn, and thrive.

When I was in high school and college, I learned several intangibles about work during my summer jobs: how to show up on time, how to work hard, how to make money at jobs that were hard labor and no fun, and how to play well with others. And I learned how to drive a forklift at the age of twelve. Additionally, I had to learn about budgeting, cash management, and taxes. These jobs included working at a lumber yard, sand blasting underground pipe in the blistering hot sun, mowing lawns for forty hours in a week, working in a meat department for a grocery store, baling hay, and walking beans.

In college, I became a resident assistant, where I was a leader in the dormitories. This job not only helped me pay for college by providing room and board, but it taught me how to deal with different types of people from around the world. I grew up in a small farming community in Iowa. (By the way, all the towns in Iowa are small farming communities.) Our population was less than 2,000 people and my graduating class was less than 90. The only diversity in people there was between those who lived in town versus those who lived on a farm. Going to college was an eye-opening experience to see students from around the world and learn about their different cultures and perspectives.

Knowledge Drop

The state of Iowa has 99 counties. According to the 2020 Census, the largest county has just under a half million people, which is twice as large as the next biggest county. The smallest county has a population of 3,704.

My first real job after college was with a trucking company. After the management training program in Arkansas, I was given my new assignment which was based in California. That's right! Small town Iowa boy was heading for California, with all that sunshine, beautiful weather, and sandy beaches. However, that was not the California where I went. I moved to the San Joaquin Valley in central California where there is a lot of agriculture, excruciatingly hot summers, and no beaches. Although I lived about an hour from the Bay Area in Northern California, our landscape looked nothing like the beautiful California I had dreamt of. Don't get me wrong, this was actually a pretty good place to live, just not the California I dreamt about as a kid.

My "office" was in an old trailer with no running water, parked in a dirt lot next to our customer's facility. We had one portable restroom between the four of us in the office. When I say portable restroom, I mean a plastic outhouse, KYBO, porta-john, outdoor loo, or porta-potty. When it rained, the area around the entire trailer flooded and we needed to walk to the front door on top of pallets so we wouldn't get our shoes wet. When it didn't rain, the dirt from the farmland next door would get kicked up, creating a big dust bowl in and around our office. Another tidbit is we were required to wear neck ties. The good news is we had air conditioning and our office was near a Jack-in-the-Box, so we got to smell that all day when the wind blew just right.

Below is an actual picture of the office trailer. Note the flooding and pallets on the ground leading to the stairs. Our "bathroom" is off to the right, just out of the picture frame.

I know the president of our division was embarrassed about our facilities, as he should have been. In fact, right after I accepted my new assignment, I went to my Arkansas apartment and packed up all my belongings for my big move to California. I shoved everything I owned in a small U-Haul trailer that was towed behind my Chevy Lumina. For whatever reason, the last thing I had to pack was my phone. And when I say phone, I mean the one that had a cord connected to a phone line in the wall. Google it. Or go to the Smithsonian. Anyway, I literally was reaching to unplug the phone when it rang. It was the division president saying he might move our offices to Los Angeles due to the poor facilities in Northern California, but he needed more time to make his decision. So, I was driving from Arkansas west toward California, not knowing where I would end up living. He decided upon leaving the terminal in Northern California, so I went.

Even with all the uncertainty and the terrible office environment, I learned a lot in that job, and it paid dividends for me. With that company, I moved five times to four different states and became one of the youngest terminal managers in their history. What did I learn? Many things, but I will narrow it down to three. First, many times, success starts with very humble beginnings. Make the best of it. Secondly, if you show your bosses that you are dedicated and loyal even if the circumstances are not the greatest, you will be rewarded. But keep in mind that there should always be a line in the sand surrounding poor circumstances. If they are illegal or unethical then you should leave the company. Third, a lot of times work is not glamorous, but it makes for a great story.

An additional benefit to being with that company is that I worked with a lot of great people. Two of those people ended up being two of the best bosses I have ever had in my career. They were influential when I worked for them and became advisors to me after I moved on. They both impacted me in different but

> **Knowledge Drop**
>
> The first U.S. patent for a polyethylene plastic portable restroom was issued in the 1960s to George Harding. The patent described a portable toilet cabana that would be made from a rigid plastic rather than wood or metal.

important ways. You need those positive influences in your life to help you navigate your career and personal life in the best possible way.

So, when you find yourself in a job that requires you to work in a dirt lot office trailer with no running water, and an outhouse for a bathroom, make the best of it because you never know how it will turn out.

Could I have left my job because of the poor working conditions in that trailer? Easily. Am I glad I did not? Absolutely. If I had left the company prematurely, would it have changed the path of my career? Probably – and not necessarily for the better. Would I have put up with that scenario later in my career? Probably not.

Looking back, I would not change a minute of my time spent in that job because of the wisdom and opportunities I gained. However, working in that office every day was not easy and certainly not clean or sanitary. It was a big inconvenience. Just because a job is inconvenient or not fun all the time doesn't mean you should jump ship at the first opportunity. Every job has its good days and bad days. Every job has its good supervisors and bad supervisors. Every job has good colleagues and bad colleagues. Most times, you need to stick it out and learn. And sometimes you must pee in a KYBO.

With that said, there are also certain times when you should leave a job, and leave it quickly. If you are ever working at a company where there is a culture of harassment, discrimination, or other illegal or unethical behavior, find the door as soon as you can. You should never work for an organization where the employees, customers, and vendors are not treated fairly and with respect.

Unfortunately, I have seen bad behavior too many times during my career. But I learned something new every single time it happened. I took a job with a small company where I had an opportunity to wear many different hats and gain new knowledge. The job was in a city where we wanted to live, and it was an exciting move. But soon after I began work, I realized the company was having financial troubles. I just did not know how bad they were.

The company offered a 401k retirement plan. We will discuss this more later, but the way it works is you determine how much money you want to divert from your paycheck and invest it in a retirement savings account. Your employer takes the money out of your paycheck and sends it to the company in charge of the retirement plan investments.

One weekend, I was reviewing my retirement plan to see how my investments were doing. Back then, you received statements in the mail either monthly or quarterly, showing all the details of your plan including the balance, investment performance, and how much money you had diverted into the plan. While looking through the paperwork, I noticed something very curious. There were not any transactions where my money was invested into the plan during that period. It was curious because I knew there was money coming out of my paycheck, but for some reason it was not showing on my statements as being deposited into my retirement account.

I dug into it further and talked to the company's management. They admitted they were removing money from my paycheck designated for the 401k plan but were not actually writing checks to the 401k plan company so it would be invested for me. They were using it to help pay company bills. I was loaning the company money without my knowledge because the company needed the cash. It was a substantial deceit, and I was very disappointed. And mad. Call it theft, embezzlement, or unethical behavior and you would be right on all fronts. They wrote me a check to make me whole and I found an opportunity to leave the company soon after.

What did I learn from this experience? **First, always make sure to monitor your paycheck.** Ensure you are being paid properly and whatever money you have coming out of your check gets put in the right places. Beyond the rare potential for theft, sometimes errors can happen, and you should watch over your money.

Second, from that day forward, I created Management Rule #1 for me and anyone who worked for me to follow: "Never mess with people's paychecks." The easiest way to lose the respect of an employee is by messing up their paycheck. Now, mistakes happen, and payroll can be complicated. However, when those mistakes do happen, companies should respond quickly and accordingly. If a company consistently does not treat you with respect by paying you correctly, treat it as a red flag that you may want to move on.

The third lesson was that not all jobs are created equal. The hard part in your career is to identify those difficult times where you should stick it out because opportunity, more responsibility, and more money is just around the corner from times where you need to move on to a new company.

If not done properly, moving from company to company can stagnate your career and your paycheck. Businesses spend large amounts of money trying to recruit, hire, and train employees so if they see a person who jumps from job to job frequently, they may be concerned with your commitment. Have patience with your career and try to make employment decisions by looking at your big picture goals instead of being driven by emotion in the moment.

However, it is okay to be a bit impatient by pushing yourself to learn new skills and wanting more responsibility so you can move up within a company to earn bigger paychecks. With that said, if the time comes where opportunities no longer exist for advancement or you are no longer happy or challenged within your current company, you must evaluate when it's time to leave.

> **Knowledge Drop**
>
> According to a U.S. Bureau of Labor Statistics about employee tenure published in 2020, the median number of years workers had been with their current employer was 4.1 years. In 1983, the number was 3.5 years and has trended upward since.

The reality is that sometimes you must leave a job or a company to make the biggest gains in the size of your paycheck. If another company recruits you, they may be more willing to entice you with a larger paycheck and lure you away from your current company. This can cause your current employer to match your increased rate of pay. It's always nice to be wanted, especially by two separate companies, but don't intentionally get into bidding wars for your services between a company you currently work for and a new company. This puts your current company in an awkward position, and if this becomes a regular routine just to get pay raises, it's time to leave. At some point, your current company will question your loyalty and if that is the only way to get a pay increase, it's time to move on.

As we have discussed, your paycheck is only one of many aspects of a job, but it's a big one. It's always a good idea to evaluate how your salary compares to other people doing your same job. Talk with competitors, colleagues, human resource managers within the industry, and utilize online resources to ensure your pay is equivalent to your value. There are several resources available, including salary.com and payscale.com which can help you understand your market value. None of these resources are exact, but they will help you understand an acceptable salary range for your current or new job. This process can also evaluate whether a job offer is fair which can help as a basis for negotiations over pay and benefits.

Before deciding to leave a company, evaluate your decision with the following thoughts:

- Do I have another job secured?
- Will my new job offer me a better work environment where I can grow and thrive to the betterment of my career?
- How will a new job help with my career path compared to my current job?
- What are the strengths and weaknesses of my current job and my new job?
- Which company will challenge me and give me the biggest advantage toward my career goals?
- Any chance I will have to pee in a KYBO during the workday?

Chapter 13

Get a Job as a Teenager

Kids are busy today. Between schoolwork, extracurricular activities, school sports, club sports, spending time with friends, and studying for the SAT before taking it three times to improve their score, kids have little extra time on their hands.

Our job as parents is to raise good citizens of the world. Being a good citizen means making a positive impact on society. A positive impact can be realized in many ways, such as treating others with respect, helping those who are less fortunate or in need, reducing your negative environmental impact on the world, and contributing to the constant improvement of your neighborhood. Another way is to be a great worker.

The positive impact of great workers can be seen throughout the world. They create, build, and sell products that consumers want and need. They drive productivity within companies so they can sell products and services for a profit. Profits are used to pay salaries and benefits for employees. Company profits also provide tax revenues for our government, which help the country thrive and develop. Profits also are used as a reinvestment within companies so they can grow by developing new products and services that make our lives easier. In turn, when companies grow, they create more jobs because they need more people to build and sell their products and services.

Great workers create new and life-changing ideas that influence the world. Think about the hard-working and intelligent people who created inventions that have changed history: electricity, light bulbs, automobiles, vaccines, telephones, and personal computers. Then think about the people who had visions of new ideas and then led a group of hard-working people to realize those visions and become something great. In recent times, those innovations were developed by employees at companies such as Microsoft, Apple, Google, and Amazon. Take a moment and look around you right now. I am willing to bet that within your close surroundings you will see a product or service impacted by one or all of these four companies. That success and innovation happened because workers made it happen.

It all happens with people who work, so a perfect place to start to be a great worker is as a teenager. The experience you gain during those first jobs will help you be a better worker in the future. You will learn how to find available jobs, build a resume, fill out applications, and experience the art of interviewing. You will learn first-hand about minimum wage, payroll taxes, and direct deposit along with the skills of what it's like to show up for work on time, punch a time clock, take direction from a supervisor, dress appropriately, and how to treat customers properly. Your steady paychecks allow you to experience the process of making money, saving money, and spending money.

I don't care if your first job is bussing tables at a fast-food restaurant, bagging groceries, selling popcorn at the local movie theater, or as a sign flipper on the corner. Those jobs are an important part of your education. It's part of making you a good citizen.

After high school, college, or vocational school, you need to be ready to work on your chosen career so that you can make money to support yourself. If you make money to support yourself and stand on your own two feet without help from others, then you become a taxpayer and a philanthropist for local causes. That is being a good citizen. With that said, at various times in your life you may need some financial help because of unforeseen circumstances. Ask for it and take it – whether it be for unemployment benefits from your government or a short-term loan from your parents. However, those situations should be an exception and not the rule on how to manage your financial future.

Money Decree
Take responsibility for your financial future. Do not rely on your family, friends, or the government to help you.

For various reasons, many kids are not expected to get jobs during their teenage years compared to when I grew up. But consider that if you don't work as a teenager, you are missing a golden opportunity to gain a critical piece of education that will help you in adulthood. The best way to get better at something is to practice. The best way to practice being a great worker is to get a job at the first opportunity.

My oldest daughter began her first real job soon after she received her driver's license. Within a few weeks of starting that job, she learned about all the things I talked about above. But she also learned some things that are difficult to teach unless you experience them for yourself. She had to talk with her supervisor about the number of hours she could work so she was able to maintain her grades in school. She had to learn how to handle it when she was called into work unexpectedly. She had to work all weekend, which consisted of two 10-hour shifts. She worked with customers who were sometimes unhappy with the quality of services. She worked with other workers who sometimes didn't treat each other with respect.

I am sure both my kids get tired of me preaching about how to be a great worker. I point out lessons at every opportunity, such as when we are standing at the local coffee shop trying to give our order to a worker who is more interested in talking with their coworker than us. That's a lesson. When you are at work, you are not there to socialize, especially when customers need service.

Then there was the time we were standing in a grocery store while two employees discussed very loudly (and with inappropriate language) how much they hated their jobs, while standing in the middle of an aisle full of customers. That's a lesson.

I am sure many of you have been to a park owned by Disney, or know of their standards for customer service. Many years ago, I attended an event where the guest speaker was previously the head of human resources for Disney. He spoke about never letting the customer "behind the curtain." Disney cast members, aka Cinderella, Pluto, and Mickey, were coached and trained that when they were in full view of customers, they were to remain in character. If they had a beef with a coworker – handle it behind the curtain. If they need to make a change to their schedule – handle it behind the curtain. When it was time for a break – handle it behind the curtain. Can you imagine seeing Snow White taking a smoke break right in the middle of the park while telling kids to leave her alone because she was on break?

When our kids were very young, we took them to Disneyland. Both were in strollers at the time. We were walking through the park and about 25 feet away, Snow White was making a bee line for a door leading her behind the curtain. It was obvious to me she was done with her shift or ready for a break. My oldest daughter sat in awe as the princess strolled by, fully in character. Just before she reached the door, she stopped and turned her attention in our direction and blew a kiss to my daughter. She could have very easily walked through the door and ignored my daughter. However, she knew how to be a good worker. She knew that little interactions like that are what build the aura of Disney.

Then there was the time we visited a big box store. While walking near the cash registers, a worker pulled off her apron and yelled to another employee, "I am outta here!" before walking into the break room to clock out of her shift. I looked at my daughter and shook my head, acknowledging another lesson. We bought our things and headed for the exit. As we approached the door, right in front of us was the worker who was very happy to be done with her workday. I watched her walk into an expansive parking lot and get in her car. The car was parked right outside the door in the very first parking spot, under a beautiful shade tree. Oh, the lessons to be learned here. A business is in business to offer products and services to customers. That means customers get the best parking spots, including those next to the front door and those with shade from the hot Arizona summer sun. Employees get the parking spots in places that are not as convenient. I must have tried to teach this lesson to my kids too often, because now when I bring it up I get a response from my teenage daughters in a tone only teenage daughters can speak: "I know, Dad! I won't park by the front door!" My job here is done.

You cannot teach these things in a classroom, or a book, or through lectures from your parents. You need to experience them yourself to become a better worker. Over time, better workers are rewarded with more responsibility and greater opportunity for advancement, which means bigger paychecks. If those paychecks are handled correctly, you move up the Financial Pyramid.

PART III

SAVING MONEY

Chapter 14
Put an Emphasis on Saving Money

Saving money can be hard. It is putting money aside and not touching it until you need it for its intended use. Why save? You save money to create more money. However, the hardest thing about having money in your pocket or bank account is not spending it. Having the means, ability, and discipline to save money will determine whether you will build wealth and move up the Financial Pyramid. Saving money properly provides financial security.

According to a 2019 survey done by GoBankingRates.com, 69% of the respondents said they had less than $1,000 in a savings account. That is an incredibly scary statistic. Worse, this survey was completed when the economy was doing well and most people who wanted to be employed had an opportunity to be employed. Sometimes these surveys and the statistics they produce can be misleading because of how many people were surveyed, who was surveyed, how they were surveyed, or the definition of a savings account. So let's just focus on this: without question, we need to put a greater emphasis on saving money.

Depending on your age and current situation, your purpose for saving can be vastly different. The older you get, the more savings you need and the more complicated your financial situation becomes. As a pre-teen, you may save money from your allowance or other odd jobs for clothes, video games, or a special ice cream treat. As you enter your teen years and your opportunity for income increases, you may save for gas money, going out to eat with your friends, and expenses for college.

After you graduate from high school and/or a post high school education, your savings should turn towards saving for big purchases such as a car or house, along with more long-term savings for retirement. When you start a family, you have all the previous savings needs, but add in a bigger need to ensure you can handle an unexpected emergency such as a car repair bill, medical bill, or loss of income.

Part II of the book helped you understand the income side of the equation (the Comes-inta), and Part IV will talk about the expense side of the equation (the Goes-outta), and this part is about the difference between the two. Everything that is left between the Comes-inta and Goes-outta should be saved for one reason or another.

> **Money Decree**
>
> Living below your means, means living without short term wants.

There are several keys to keep in mind to save successfully:

- It is NEVER too early or too late to start saving. But the earlier the better.
- Control your expenses to live within your means, which includes meeting your savings goals.
- Make savings a habit and part of your regular routine, just like brushing your teeth. Move money to your savings every time you get paid and watch it grow.
- Be disciplined about saving and spending. Have a plan and follow it.

The rest of this part will discuss different reasons to save, how much you should save, and where to save. In the following chapters, we will discuss this in more detail, but let's start by understanding the risk versus reward concept when saving money.

There are a vast number of ways to save money. Many are simplistic and come with no risk; others are more complicated and come with a risk of losing value in your savings. The riskier your investment, the greater the opportunity for a bigger gain or a bigger loss.

If you put $500 in your bank savings account, you have no risk in losing that $500 and you will only gain a very small amount of interest from the bank. If you invest $500 in the stock market, you have a much greater opportunity to make a lot of money on top of the original $500, but you also have an opportunity to lose your original $500 altogether.

Determining the savings purpose and the time frame before you need the money will help you decide how risky you should be with your savings.

Where you save your money will depend on several factors, but a big one is when you will use the money you are saving.

If you are saving money for an immediate need, such as to buy a new television set, the money should be put in a place where it is easily accessible and has no risk in losing value. This could be a savings account at the same bank where you have a checking account. There is no risk in losing your savings, but there is also very little you will gain in interest on top of the money you save.

Knowledge Drop

Why is our money green? In the 1860's green was used as an anti-counterfeiting measure. The color was still utilized in modern times because the ink was plentiful and durable, plus the color was associated with stability.

If you are saving for a retirement that is decades away, you want to place the money in a higher risk investment where you can gain a higher return over a long period of time. Retirement funds are generally invested in the stock market through mutual funds. Over short periods of time, the stock market's performance will vary greatly, but over a long period of time, the stock market will provide a good return on your investment.

According to NerdWallet, the stock market has averaged a return of 10% per year over the last thirty years. During those thirty years, there were large gains and large losses, but the average return was about 10%.

When you are saving money that you will not need for twenty or thirty years, such as retirement money, you can utilize riskier investments. This is because if you have a down year, you have a greater amount of time to gain back any losses you incurred.

This chart should provide further clarity with this concept by providing an overview of how some investments fit into a risk/reward scenario.

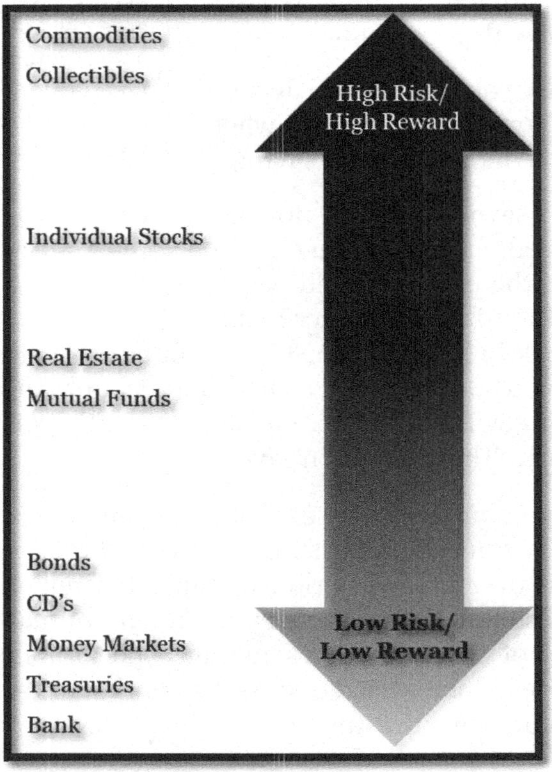

Now let's dig deeper into the specifics of saving and how it can move you up the Financial Pyramid, considering how to use the risk/reward evaluation to your advantage.

Chapter 15

Your Uh-Oh Fund and Other Short-Term Savings

Short-term savings is money you set us aside that you may need in the near term, meaning within the next twelve months.

When you are a teenager or college student, you may be saving for smaller things such as a new video game, books, clothing, or your mother's birthday gift. Bigger ticket items can include a car down payment, a vacation, college tuition, or your father's birthday gift.

As you get older and live on your own, the single most important short-term savings focus should be on an emergency fund, aka an "uh-oh" fund. An uh-oh fund is money you set aside for those inevitable uh-oh moments in life. Uh-oh, my car broke down and needs repairs. Uh-oh, my water heater failed in my house. Uh-oh, I broke my arm and I have a big hospital bill. Uh-oh, I lost my job because my company is downsizing their workforce due to a global pandemic.

According to Bankrate's Emergency Savings Survey in June of 2021, 25% of U.S. adults have no emergency savings. 26% have less than three months' worth of expenses and 25% had six months' expenses or more.

Immediately upon moving into the real world, your primary financial emphasis should be to build your uh-oh fund and maintain it for the rest of your life. Because life tends to throw unknowns at you at the least convenient times, you must plan for the unexpected. If you are not prepared, it can put a world of hurt on your finances and your life.

You can start your uh-oh fund by setting aside small amounts, even $10 or $20 per week. But just start! And *do not* touch it unless an emergency arises. To clarify further, an emergency is not an immediate need for caffeine or an annual sale at your favorite clothing store. Leave the money for real emergencies.

The ultimate size of your uh-oh fund will depend on your monthly expenses and how many people are dependent upon your income to survive. The greater your expenses and the number of people who depend on your income, the greater your uh-oh fund must be. Later, we will discuss budgeting in detail so you can identify your monthly expenses.

> **Knowledge Drop**
>
> According to the FDIC, in 2021, there are a total of 4,983 banks in the United States. So, there are plenty of places to store your short-term savings.

If you currently do not have an uh-oh fund, your initial goal should be to have at least three months of your expenses set aside. Then build it to six months. Eventually, you should have a year's worth of expenses sitting in reserve, especially if you are supporting a family that would be in dire straits without your income.

When you have an uh-oh fund, it removes a lot of financial pressure when that unexpected issue arises. I have lost my job twice during my career, meaning my employer asked me to leave and never return. Both times I lost my job during poor economic times where it was tough to find a new one and neither time was it because of something I did to deserve being fired. Sometimes bad things happen to good people. Those times were very stressful but thank goodness we had our uh-oh fund in place, because it could have been a lot worse.

The first time I lost my job, we were D.I.N.K.s (double income, no kids). By no means was it a pleasant experience, but because we had an uh-oh fund and my wife was still working, we could have lasted quite some time before financial strain took place.

The second job loss was during the Great Recession. My wife and I had two young daughters and I was the only earner. Even though we had short-term savings that would have lasted well past a year, having a family of four depend on your income takes the whole adulting thing to a brand-new level. Thankfully, we had planned for such unfortunate events. If we had not, the financial repercussions could have lasted a long time and included putting my family at risk, losing our home, or even bankruptcy.

There are several options for investing short-term savings. Due to the short time frame and immediate need of your short-term savings, it is important to only consider investments on the low risk/low reward end of the spectrum. Whether the money is for your uh-oh fund or a down payment on a car you are buying in two months, the money needs to be easily accessible and you do not want to be concerned with it losing value.

Knowledge Drop

On September 2, 1969, America's first automatic teller machine (ATM) makes its public debut, dispensing cash to customers at Chemical Bank in Rockville Centre, New York.

Short-term savings that will be needed within a short period of time, say less than a couple months, can be held in a bank's savings account where you also maintain your checking account. You will receive little or no interest income, but you will have immediate access to the funds by electronically transferring it to your checking account or withdrawing the money from an automated teller machine (ATM).

Generally, it is also a good idea to keep a portion of your uh-oh money that can be accessed immediately if an issue comes up. Typically, we keep about one month's worth of expenses in an account where we can get access to that money the same day.

All other short-term savings, including the rest of your uh-oh fund, should be kept in a money market or high yield savings account. By using these types of accounts, it offers a couple advantages over a regular bank savings account:

- The accounts are similar to a regular savings account, except they offer much better interest. For example, a regular bank may offer an interest rate of 0.01% while a money market or high yield savings account would offer 1% or 2% depending on what is happening with the economy and interest rates nationwide.
- The money is harder to touch, which means it's less likely you will want to touch it. The best money market or high yield savings accounts are online accounts where you would electronically transfer the money when you need it. Generally, this could take a day or two.

You can quickly access money in your bank savings account, either by using the ATM or by electronically transferring money into your bank checking account the same day. Money markets or high yield savings accounts can be a bit different. They are not aligned with the big, mainstream banks that have buildings on every corner in a major city. More likely than not, the best rates are found with online only banks. Some of these online banks can link directly to a checking account or debit card which can give you immediate access to your funds. Otherwise, it can take longer to move money between accounts for access, and they have standards and rules that you should research. You get a much higher interest rate, but there are some things to consider and understand, such as:

- **If you are using a high yield savings account, make sure to use a bank and account that is insured by the FDIC**, which means you will never lose your money if you have less than the insured amount in the account (which is currently $250,000). It will not lose value, and if the bank falters, the government will pay you back the money in your account. There is no risk. Just be sure to check that the bank is FDIC insured. Money markets are not FDIC insured.

- **Identify if there are rules on the number of times you can transfer money in and out of the account.** Many times, these are limited to six per month.

- **Identify how long it typically takes to move money to and from your accounts.** If you have a checking account in a different bank from your money market or savings account, then set up the account so you can link it to your checking account and transfer by way of ACH (automated clearing house). Typically transfers should only take a working day or two.

- **Identify any restrictions on the amount of money you can transfer per transaction or over a month's time.** Many times, the accounts will offer no restrictions to deposit money, but significant restrictions on moving money out of their accounts.

- **The bank may place a brief, temporary hold on the money** when you set up an account or transfer money into an account. This is a pretty common practice and should not stop you from using the bank, just know you may have a few days or a week where you won't have access to the funds you just deposited.

- **Identify the minimum amount to open an account and the balance you need to maintain in the account to avoid fees.** Sometimes banks will charge a fee if your balance drops below a certain balance or if the account becomes dormant. Other accounts may require you to have direct deposits tied to the account.

- **Pull up and review the fee schedule to see if there are any other hidden fees.** These fees can include a dormancy fee if you don't have any transactions over a year's time, transactions fees if you exceed a certain limit per month, or low balance fees if your balance drops below a certain number of an average over a month.

As a rule, you should not open accounts that make it overly hard to gain access to your money or charge you fees for a low balance. In the case of short-term savings, do not sacrifice getting quick access to your money for a higher rate of return. It is easy to find a good savings rate with a low balance requirement ($0 to $100) to open and maintain the account for free.

The internet will provide you with a plethora of options for competitive money markets or high yield savings accounts. A couple of my website preferences to evaluate current rates among several banks are Bankrate and NerdWallet. Rates change often, so it is a good idea to check once every few months to be sure you are still getting a competitive rate.

Chapter 16

I Want to Buy Something Big

After your uh-oh fund is in place, your focus can and should shift to other types of savings.

Any money you save beyond the near term should be handled differently. I'm talking about saving money for things like a down payment on a house, your kids' college funds, and retirement. This money needs to be invested somewhere higher up on the risk/reward investment scale. The longer the time frame before you need the money, the riskier you can become, because ultimately you want a higher return on your savings investment.

For this type of saving, a great option is to utilize mutual funds. A mutual fund is a common investment tool where professionals invest money for you into a fund that buys and sells a group of stocks, bonds, or money markets. Because of its diversity, mutual funds tend to be a favorite investment for all kinds of investors. But like anything in life, where there is opportunity for gain, there is an opportunity for loss. Any money invested in mutual funds isn't guaranteed and can lose value over time. However, if you look at the history of the stock market, there are always ups and downs, but long-term investments will gain value over a long period of time. You just need to invest in it correctly.

Guidance about how to invest is not the purpose of this book. Instead, I would like to show you how important it is to invest on a regular basis with a plan in mind. There are books, magazines, and financial experts who can help you invest and give you as much knowledge as you are willing to take. Spend time understanding how to invest wisely because it is a big deal. Small decisions about investing today will make a significant difference in the years to come.

If you invest correctly, over a long period of time you will have an opportunity for greater success if you follow these simple rules:

- **Start early.** As soon as you have made some headway on your emergency fund, start saving for retirement or your other long-term goals.

- **Turn on autopilot.** Set up automatic and recurring deposits into your savings and other investment accounts. This way, you won't have to remember to move money into your accounts and it will keep you from wanting to use the money for something else.

- **Let it be.** Once you invest the money, consider it out of your hands. Leave it alone and let it build over time until you get to your intended use.

- **Hands off!** Do not touch the money saved for any other purpose except for its intended use. If the money is for retirement, do not use it as a down payment on a house or as your uh-oh fund.

- **Stay the course.** The stock market will have its ups and downs. Don't panic when the market has a sharp decline. If your money is invested correctly and for a long period of time, history shows that the market will return to growth after a downturn. Also, don't go on a spending spree when there is a significant increase. Know the intended purpose of your money and stick to the plan.

- **There's no magic bullet.** There are no guarantees or shortcuts to make money quickly over the long haul. If someone is trying to sell you on an investment that guarantees a high return on the investment or an opportunity to make money quick, do not walk away – run.

- **Let it grow.** There are no shortcuts in building wealth. Invest wisely in conservative and well-known investments over a long period of time.

Chapter 17

What the Heck is Compounding Interest? – Saving for the Long Term

One of the key rules in successful long-term investing is to start investing your money early in life. It doesn't matter if you start with as little as $25 per month: just start now. By starting early and allowing your funds to grow over a long time, you'll have a greater chance for a big balance of funds to use for long term savings goals, such as your kid's college fund or your retirement. Why? Because you will take advantage of compounding interest.

Compounding interest can be explained using simple math. If on January 1 of this year you invest $100 in an account that earns 6% interest, on December 31 you will have $106 from your original $100 investment. Next year, the exact same thing happens, but the difference is you earn 6% on $106 instead of $100 like you did last year. At the end of the second year, your account will have grown to $112.36. You are gaining interest on top of interest. The interest you gain is compounded exponentially because you aren't just gaining interest on your original investment, but your investment plus the interest.

If you invested $100 per month in that same account which pays you 6% interest, you would have $16,470 from your investment of $12,000 at the end of ten years. This is the power of compounding interest. The key is to start as early as you can and invest as much as you can, for as long as you can.

Let's look at another example by comparing the investment strategies of three different people. First, there is Mike, who is very savvy with money, a real go-getter, and easy on the eyes. From the age of **25** until he was **35**, he invested $100 per month in an account that paid 6% interest. After he stopped contributing the $100 a month, he left the money in the same account and continued to earn a 6% return.

Secondly, there is Jen who is stunningly beautiful, extremely wise, and surprisingly patient with her husband, who happens to be Mike. She began investing $100 per month at the age of **35** and stopped at **45**. After she stopped contributing, she too left her money in the same account that paid 6% interest.

Third, there is Simon, who was too busy spending all his money on expensive craft beers and taking tango lessons early in life. He did not start investing his $100 per month until he was **45** and continued until he was **65** years old.

Mike and Jen both invested a total of $12,000 over their 10 years of respective investing. The only difference is that Mike started his investing ten years before Jen did. Simon invested twice as much and started twenty years after Mike and ten years after Jen.

The value in each of their accounts at the age of 65 is as follows:

Mike =$99,191
Jen = $54,850
Simon = $46,768

Are you surprised? Well, you shouldn't be. This is a book about personal finance, and you should have guessed I was trying to make a point and the numbers would be skewed. Anyway, Simon invested twice as much as both Mike and Jen, but his account is half as much as Mike's. Even Jen made a significant amount lower than Mike by waiting ten years to begin investing.

Below is a graph showing a comparison of the three scenarios from the age of 25 until 65.

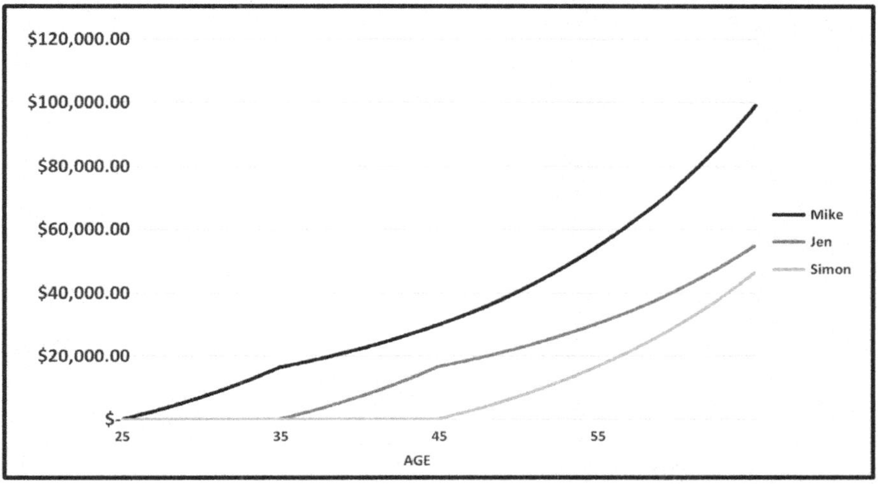

The point is clear. To achieve the greatest gain on your investment, use time and compounding interest to your benefit. As they used to say in Chicago during election time, "Vote early and vote often." The same is true for investing – invest early and invest often.

Chapter 18

Pay Yourself First!

As you get older, financial lives get more complicated. Expenses typically increase along with your income. You tend to buy more expensive things, such as cars and homes. Plus, there are various burdens on your income to pay for those increased expenses and to support others in your life. There can be long term relationships, marriages, and children who create a significant strain on your income. These complexities can make it hard to prioritize your long-term savings goals. Money gets pulled in different directions and it's important to have a plan.

Becoming a parent is one of the most proud and exhilarating times during your life (despite the sleepless nights when they are babies and tests of your patience when they are teenagers). You want the best for your children in every facet of their lives and it is easy to put their needs before yours. In most cases, that's fine – except when we talk about your financial future.

Your children will be just fine without the latest cell phone, tablet, gaming device, or other expensive things. Spending lavishly on your children may make you feel happy at the time, but it can easily derail your own financial future, and not provide good financial training for them either. Teach your children well by prioritizing your spending needs and following a plan. No child benefits by getting things handed to them without hard work, appreciation, and the knowledge of how finances work. This includes how you pay for college.

The lesson to remember is to pay yourself first. Simplistically, this means as you get older, your order of financial priority should be

1) emergency uh-oh fund,

2) your retirement,

3) your kid's college fund.

Pay yourself first by funding your uh-oh fund to take care of the unexpected life events. Then, save money for your retirement so you can take full advantage of time and compounding interest and maximize your savings. Last, but certainly not least, take care of the needs of your kids for college or vocational school.

Think about it this way: If your kids have a fully funded plan to go to college, but you must work until you're ninety or die before you can retire (pun intended), that does not sound like a good life – at least not to me. Fund your retirement, then focus on your kids. There are other options available to fund college or post-secondary education that aren't available for retirement. Your kids can get scholarships, grants, or loans. They can even save up on their own through jobs before and during college. I have never found anyone that will give me a scholarship, grant, or loan so I can retire. Pay yourself first.

In Chapter 15, we discussed how to fund your uh-oh fund. In the next chapter, we will discuss options to fund your kid's future education expenses. For the rest of this chapter, let's focus in on how to save for retirement.

There are several options to consider when saving for retirement. An emphasis should be given to those accounts that have tax shelter advantages. A tax shelter is a legal strategy to lower your income taxes. With retirement, there are certain accounts that provide an overall tax benefit through either your deposits into an account, through the growth of an account, or with both. Tax laws change frequently, so be sure to do some research on the current laws, so you have the most up-to-date information.

Also know that this money is for retirement and nothing else. Put the money in your retirement accounts on a regular and automated basis so you can leave it there and allow it to grow. Tax sheltered retirement accounts give you opportunities to remove the money for various reasons in addition to retirement. However, when you remove the money before a specific age – usually before you turn 59½ - there are severe tax penalties associated with an early withdrawal. Just think about it as a lockbox that cannot be opened until you are ready to retire and at least 59½ years old.

Here is a listing of the most common types of retirement accounts and how each can benefit your retirement planning. They are listed in order of priority based on the most effective ways to save for retirement.

401k Retirement Plans

The most popular retirement plan offered by employers is a 401k, which is a quick and easy path to start saving money for retirement in a tax-efficient way. When you sign up for a 401k, pre-tax money is automatically taken from your paycheck by your employer and put into mutual funds on your behalf. You can pick the mutual funds you want, or many 401k plans will help do it for you. A lot of employers will also match a portion of your contribution as a benefit to you. For example, a company may say they will match half of what you contribute to the 401k, up to 5%. If you defer 5% of your paycheck into the 401k, the company will add half of that number (another 2.5%) to your account. If you put in 7%, the company still puts in 2.5% because that is the maximum they will contribute. If you put in 2%, the

> **Knowledge Drop**
>
> The 401k retirement plans are named after the section of IRS tax code which governs them. They were developed by the government in the 1980's to help Americans save for their retirement.

company will match half of it, or 1%. The company match is free money to you and is an excellent benefit you should take full advantage of. Determine the matching amount offered by your company and ensure you are at least contributing to maximize the match.

Sometimes you need to work for the company a few years to be fully "vested" in the company match money. In other words, the company generally wants you to work for them for a while before they will give you full ownership of the money they contributed to your 401k. An example of a company's vesting period could be an employee receives 20% ownership of the employer contributions after one year of employment, 60% after two years, and 100% after three years. The company is trying to entice you to stay with them longer so they can get a return on the investment they made in you. If you leave before your account is fully vested, they will deduct the matching funds (and the earnings associated with it) from your account. The funds you place into the 401k are always owned by you and are always fully vested.

Each calendar year, there is a maximum amount you can contribute to your 401k. There are other rules for a 401k, but the maximum amount is the big one. The government wants to restrict how much money you put into this tax shelter because it reduces your income taxes paid to them. They will help you shelter some, but they still need tax money from you.

Knowledge Drop

According to Vanguard's "How America Saves 2021" report, the average 401k plan balances reached $129,157 in 2020, up from $78,276 in 2011.

For example, in 2022 the maximum amount you can contribute to your 401k is $20,500, if you are under fifty. If you are fifty or older, you are eligible for catch-up contributions that are an additional $6,500. The catch-up contributions allow older workers to defer additional money into their accounts in case they did not start saving for retirement until later in life. By doing this, the government helps you catch up by allowing you to contribute more to your accounts. However, even though you should take advantage of the catch-up contributions if you can, this is not a great strategy and does not give you permission to start retirement saving late. As we discussed earlier, starting your saving early is the single biggest contributing factor to your success. Even though later in life the law allows you to contribute more, you already lost the advantage of time. In truth, it's nearly impossible to actually catch up. Also, this assumes you will have the available funds to maximize the catch-up contribution feature.

Funds in a 401k can be withdrawn after the age of 59½ without a penalty. There are certain features of a 401k where you can withdraw funds when you are younger than 59½ without a penalty, but you are required to pay back the money to your 401k or pay taxes on the withdrawal. These withdrawals are determined because of a financial hardship that can be related to unpaid medical expenses, a tax bill, educational costs, or expenses related to a primary home. One of those commonly used features is to use a 401k loan for a down payment on a house. Even though this feature is available to you, and may seem appealing, I strongly advise you to resist that urge.

When you remove money from your 401k for a down payment, you can do it without a penalty, but this transaction is similar to a loan. You must pay back the money to your 401k with interest, which is being paid to yourself. Even though that sounds like a great deal, there are some significant downsides:

- By removing that money from your 401k, it no longer can increase in value because you removed it from the investment. That is called an opportunity cost. You lost the opportunity to gain earnings because the money was no longer invested. It cost you the gain you would have had if the money was still in your 401k.
- If you miss any repayments, it could trigger a tax penalty on your withdrawal.
- If you leave your job, you must repay the loan in its entirety, instead of making payments, or it could trigger a tax penalty on your withdrawal.

This is retirement money, not down payment money. Keep your buckets of money separate from each other and you are more likely to achieve your financial goals.

If you work for a government agency, they offer plans very similar to a 401k but without employer matching opportunities. They are called 403b or 457 plans.

How to Contribute to a 401k

Participating in a 401k retirement plan is very easy and requires a limited number of decisions. Since they are offered through your employer, they will determine which company will administer the 401k for you, which funds will be offered, and all the rules relating to how much they will match.

You determine the amount you want to invest and where you want to invest it. Many 401k companies will also help you determine the best funds for you based on your age and time to retire. It's okay to listen to their advice but do your own research and ensure you agree with what they are telling you before you just blindly invest your hard-earned funds.

Individual Retirement Account (IRA)

If a 401k retirement plan is not available to you, or if you are fortunate enough to max out your contribution, look to a Traditional or Roth IRA. Tax laws pertaining to IRAs change often, so be sure to research which one works for you.

The contribution limits are much lower than a 401k and generally change annually. In 2022, the maximum contribution is $6,000, with a catch-up contribution (similar to the 401k) for those age fifty and older of $1,000. These contributions are limited for high income earners.

Here is an overview showing the key differences between a Roth IRA and Traditional IRA:

Roth IRA	**Traditional IRA**
Contribute with post tax money	Contribute with pre or post-tax money
Money grows tax free	Money grows tax deferred
Can withdraw at age 59 ½ penalty and tax free for retirement	Can withdraw at age 59 ½ and taxed at based on your income at that time
Can withdraw for college expenses tax-free	May provide annual tax benefit

<u>How to Contribute to an IRA</u>

IRAs give you more flexibility because you can choose which company to work with and where to invest your funds. My recommendation is to use a low-cost company such as Vanguard or Fidelity. They have excellent online resources, easy-to-use websites, and a plethora of investments to choose from at a reasonable price.

After you choose a company, go to their website, open an IRA account, and invest in **no-load mutual funds**.

A **mutual fund** is a professionally managed investment that pools money from many investors and purchases stocks, bonds, money markets, and/or other assets from many different organizations on your behalf.

> **Knowledge Drop**
>
> According to the Statista Research Department, in 2019 there were a total of 7,945 mutual funds in the United States.

A **no-load mutual fund** is when you are not charged any sales fees or commissions just to buy or sell the mutual fund. However, each fund has a fee that is charged for administration of the mutual fund. Pay particular attention to these fees before buying a mutual fund because while they may seem low, they can easily add up over time. Most websites will show you how well a particular mutual fund has performed over time with and without the fees included in the calculation.

Mutual fund companies do the research and legwork on which company stocks to buy based on the goal of their fund. Mutual funds are less risky than buying stock with one specific company such as McDonald's or Coca Cola, because instead of owning just one stock, a mutual fund owns many different stocks. In fact, the typical mutual fund will own stocks in at least fifteen or twenty different companies. This type of diversification helps reduce risk and allows you to own investments across various industries and business sizes by owning a single mutual fund.

A mutual fund is a simple way to diversify your risk among many different companies, but remember, with any investment there is always risk. There are no guarantees when you invest in the stock market, but with consistent contributions and solid investment strategies over time, your retirement funds should grow and thrive.

Taxable Accounts

If you have put the maximum amounts in your 401k or equivalent retirement account and/or IRAs, and still can save even more, then you can open an additional account that does not have any tax protection or maximum contribution limits. Due to the taxes, this only makes sense after you have fully taken advantage of the tax-sheltered accounts.

How to Contribute

Approach your taxable accounts just like you would the IRAs, but set them up as a taxable account. Find low cost, no-load mutual funds that meet your needs and start your investing.

Any of these accounts can be set up in minutes, not hours. But take time to investigate the right mutual funds for you, considering the mutual funds goals and their fees. You can even set up recurring deposits into these accounts just like you would a 401k contribution from your paycheck.

I hope this information was helpful for you to understand how to invest. But your next question is probably how much you should invest in these retirement accounts. While I can't give you personal, individual advice about your situation, here are some tips in broad strokes about maximizing your retirement savings. You can start using any of these tips today.

Tip #1

At a ***minimum***, contribute enough into your employer's 401k retirement plan to maximize the employer's matching contribution. **I can't stress this enough: that's free money they are giving you.** If your employer matches half of your contribution up to 5%, then at a minimum put in 5% to get their full match.

This is exactly like that $20 bill you found on the sidewalk you were so happy about earlier. Do not step over it. Grab every single dollar they leave on the sidewalk for you. They are helping you fund your retirement as an added benefit of working for the company and it should be considered as important as your regular rate of pay.

Tip #2

Just so we're clear, contributing the minimum amount only applies early in your career when your earnings are generally at their lowest levels. As you build your career and increase your income, the expectation should be higher. Much higher.

Tip #3

Every time you get a raise, put at least half of that raise toward your retirement account. If you get a raise of 5%, then you should increase your 401k contribution by 2.5% *at a minimum*. Same thing goes for bonuses or unexpected cash delivered to your doorstep. A *minimum* of half of that money should go toward your retirement account, if not more.

Tip #4

Your ultimate goal is to put at least twenty percent of your salary toward savings accounts, most of which should be allocated for retirement. I know that seems like a shocking number and feels unattainable, but it can be done. By working through the tips in this book, you can move toward maximizing your savings rate, watching your retirement accounts grow, and moving up the Financial Pyramid.

Tip #5

Increase your retirement savings starting immediately. If you aren't participating in your employer's 401k, then start tomorrow. If you are participating, I want to congratulate you, but then ask you to increase your contribution by 1%, 2%, or more. Every little bit makes an impact.

Some Retirement Contribution Math

Let's assume you are currently making $50,000 and you are contributing 5% to your 401k plan. If you get paid every two weeks, that means you are currently contributing a pre-tax amount of $96.15 every paycheck to the 401k.

If you increase your contribution by 1%, your contribution to the 401k will increase by $19.23, but your paycheck will only decrease by about $16 or so. By a show of hands, how many of you would pay $16 to get $19 in return? Come on, raise your hand. I see you holding out. You know I'm right!

> **Knowledge Drop**
>
> According to the Iben Institute of Income and Financial Studies (IIIFS) of the Greater Phoenix Area**, 5 out of 5 people would pay $16 to get $19.
>
> **This is a joke.

How is it possible that you pay $19 into your 401k, but it only costs you $16? Remember when we covered how pre-tax deductions impact your check back in Chapter 10? Check it out again if you need a refresher, I'll be here when you get back.

There are two things to remember about investing into a pre-tax account. First, because you're investing pre-tax, the impact on your take home pay will be less than your increased investment, because you're reducing your taxes along with increasing your investment. Secondly, small amounts matter considerably over a long period of time.

To show my point about the latter, let's pretend that you are currently 25 years old and you are going to make $60,000 for the rest of your life. I really hope that's not true, and these could be terrible assumptions about your age and income, but I am the one creating this imaginary world. Bear with me, here.

The graph below compares three different 401k portfolios based on what percent of your income is put into the account each year. Scenario 1 shows 12% of your $60,000 income being put in the 401k and your account will be worth over $1.2 million at the age of 65. Scenario 2 assumes 6% of your income and would allow you to

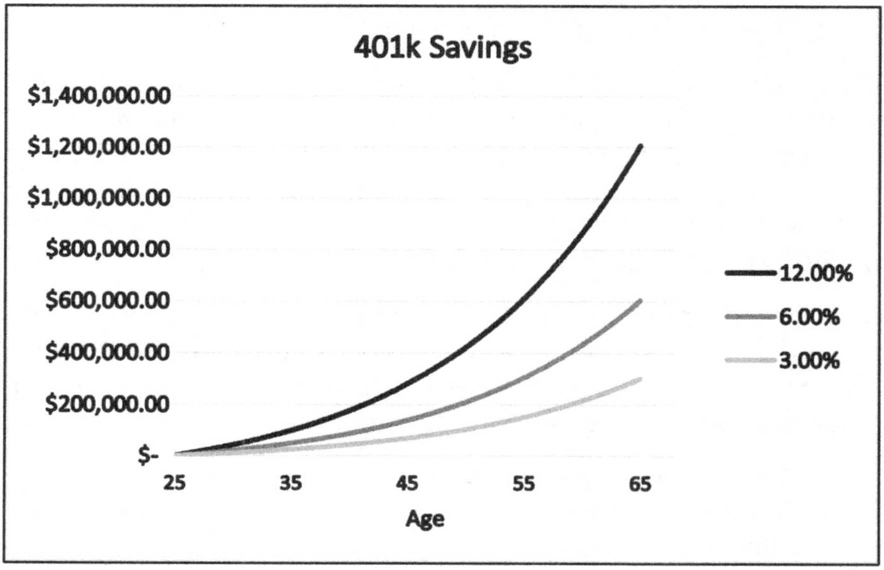

achieve over $600,000 in that same time. Scenario 3 details a 3% deferral and would put your account at about $300,000.

This graph projects you will make $60,000 every year during this forty-year stretch, and you'll make the same 6% growth on your investment every year. None of those things will actually happen as shown, but that isn't the point. Your income will fluctuate, the rate of return goes up and down, and everyone's investment timeline is different. This graph shows how important it is to start to invest early, invest consistently, and maximize your contribution. Over forty or more years of investing, small changes will make a huge impact.

Let's Talk About Social Security

One of the many programs developed during and because of the Great Depression is the Social Security Act of 1935. During that time, many Americans lost all financial security due to a collapse of the economy. People lost jobs and their entire savings, if they had any. The government wanted to provide certain protection (or insurance) to elderly or disabled Americans who were at significant risk without steady income. Therefore, they created Social Security.

The program is basically funded two ways. First, you pay a tax with a percentage of each paycheck into Social Security, and secondly, your employer matches your tax amount. This acts very similarly to any other type of insurance. You pay a tax (instead of a premium) and the money is set aside for those that either need it or have reached a certain age to receive the benefits.

Over time, the program has changed, but the basic premise remains about the same. According to the Social Security Administration, "The Social Security Act and related laws establish a number of programs that have the following basic purposes:

- To provide for the material needs of individuals and families;
- To protect aged and disabled persons against the expenses of illnesses that may otherwise use up their savings;

- To keep families together; and
- To give children the chance to grow up healthy and secure."

I bring up Social Security for a couple of reasons. First, to show the description above about the true purpose of Social Security. Nowhere does it say the purpose is to fully fund your retirement. If you pay a Social Security tax, then you deserve the benefits of Social Security when that time comes. But, under no circumstances should you believe that your Social Security benefits will be a financial windfall to allow a secure retirement. That was never the purpose of Social Security, nor will it ever be.

Secondly, I would advise you to never count on Social Security as a part of your retirement funding. Social Security is a hot political topic for various reasons. The government has a hard time collecting money from you for a specific purpose, and not spending it on a totally different purpose. Along with the fact that as more baby boomers retire, the funds expenses are increasing, so the future of Social Security is at risk.

Knowledge Drop

According to the Social Security Administration the total assets were $2.91 trillion at the end of 2020, and the trust fund reserves are projected to become fully exhausted in 2037.

Politicians will generally find a way to solve the problem, but that could change the way the program looks and works at some point in the future. Changes can include the amount people are taxed and the age at which retirees can draw from the fund. This has been going on for as long as I can remember, and early on I took the position that I should never count on ever receiving any of that money back. I would advise you to do the same. Then, if it gets rescued during a time when you need it (or earn it), Social Security will be an unplanned gift.

Chapter 19

Now Help Your Kids with College

Ok, kids. Not that I am rushing you to have kids of your own – in fact, please wait until I am mentally ready to be a grandfather. I will let you know when that is. Don't call me; I'll call you.

Let's talk about saving for your kid's college. As I told you many times, I had to pay my own way through college, I walked to school in six inches of snow with hundred-mile-an-hour winds, and a windchill of minus 75. It taught me a ton. It not only taught me how to layer my clothing for maximum warmth, it taught me to value the education I was getting because it was on my own dime. I wanted a return on my investment, which took a lot of hard work and effort.

It taught me how to budget, because I didn't have a college savings fund to work with. I had to work throughout college, and I also received loans and grants. During three of those years, I worked as a resident assistant in the dormitories which provided me free room and board, along with a small stipend which I think was about fifty bucks a month.

While helping me financially, the experiences I gained from that job were unbelievable. I worked with and became a leader of students from around the world and with experiences different from mine. The job was eye-opening for me since I grew up in a small farming community where almost all the people I knew had similar backgrounds.

After I graduated, got a job, and entered the real world of being a tax-paying citizen, I had to learn how to pay off the debt I had incurred during my time in college. Even though I was able to pay a large amount of my expenses through my R.A. job and summer work, I still walked away with a good amount of debt. But it was a good debt. It was a reasonable and affordable amount for what I got in return. It paid for a great education and allowed me in the door to get great jobs and a great life. Those student loans provided a return on investment. The loans I received required me to begin monthly payments six months after graduation. I don't remember how long they gave me to pay it back, but I do remember paying it off quite early. Even though the interest rate was low for the loan, I just remember wanting it gone. I hated making those monthly payments when I knew I could use that money somewhere else.

So, with that said, here are some rules for your kid's college savings account. **First, be a little selfish.** Do not begin to save for your kid's college education until you have fully funded your uh-oh fund and saved for retirement, or until you are contributing the maximum amount allowed by law into tax deferred retirement accounts and saving a minimum of twenty percent of your income for retirement.

Secondly, paying half is better than paying all. If you can reasonably afford it, pay for no more than half of the college expenses at a school that will provide a clear return on investment. All the rest should come from scholarships, grants, and government backed loans which should be repaid by your kid.

Third, an education is an investment. Make sure that whatever higher education is chosen – 4-year college, junior college, community college, or vocational school – ensure there is a return on the investment. Any money you pay for an education should be treated as an investment. An investment is where you pay money and expect to see a return on that investment in a reasonable amount of time. You pay money for tuition, room and board, and books so that you can get a job and a career. That career needs to pay you enough money to pay off the amount you just spent on your education in a reasonable amount of time.

If you choose a school that costs $750,000 for a four-year degree and start a career that pays you $30,000 per year, that is a very poor return on your investment (ROI). Simplistically speaking, it would take you twenty-five years to recoup your investment ($750,000 cost divided by $30,000 salary). If you go to a vocational school that costs $20,000 where you can get a job immediately that pays $60,000 per year, that is an excellent return on your investment. You would recoup your investment within 4 months ($20,000 cost divided by $60,000 salary). These are extreme ends of the spectrum, but they prove my point.

Knowledge Drop

According to a College Board report, in 2020 the average cost of attending a 4-year public college with in-state tuition is $26,820 per year. A private college costs $54,880 per year.

Avoid some common pitfalls here by researching potential jobs for your chosen career path. If jobs are hard to come by in your chosen field, or you they are on the lower end of the pay spectrum, you need to change your career path, or find a lower cost education. Research can be done with some simple internet searches or talking with people currently working in your interested field of study. Learn from other people's mistakes before you make them yourself.

Parents and kids sometimes become enamored with getting into the "greatest" schools because of the prestige (and cost). There was a recent scandal where parents were paying big money to get their kids into prestigious schools even though the kids had not earned it or deserved it. Many times, I think parents' decision making can be misguided because they understandably want what they think is the very best for their kids. But that doesn't always mean they need to attend the most prestigious and expensive schools in the land. Nor should you teach your kids it's ok to cheat to get what you want.

Education is an investment that requires a return. It serves no purpose to put your kids in a position where either of you ends up with massive amounts of debt before they even have their first job.

If your kid knows what they want to do for a living – great! Find a school that teaches those skills and provides an ROI in a reasonable amount of time. More likely, if they don't know what they want to do for a living, find ways to get them a broad-based education where they can try out different classes and settle into a career without spending massive amounts of money with no return.

I had no idea what I wanted to do when I went to college. I knew it was in business, so I entered the business college. It took me about a year and a half to figure out the actual major I wanted to pursue. I received an excellent education that provided me options for my career and an excellent return on investment and I was not in so much debt that I could never recover.

A great education is what you make of it. No matter the school you attend, if you work hard and gain the knowledge and skills to be a great worker, you will come out ahead. Also know that an education at any school is not a guarantee for a great job with high wages. You have to make those things happen.

Here endeth the soap box.

An excellent way to start saving for college is with a 529 plan. A 529 plan allows you to invest in mutual funds and the earnings from the mutual funds are tax free. The money from the 529 plan must be used for post-secondary educational expenses, so be sure that is the path your child would like to take. Any other uses will be charged taxes and a penalty, so proceed cautiously. Typically, the 529 plan is in the name of your child who will use the plan, but you still own the assets. You have the flexibility of changing the beneficiary of the account if you want to transfer it to another child.

When we set up our 529 plan, we put the account in our oldest child's name, but we plan to switch it to our youngest daughter while they are both in college. They are three years apart in age, so we can use the same account for both. This allows us to have just one account that will help handle both of their college expenses instead of opening an account for each and having to be strategic about how much each of them will need.

Some states offer 529 plans that give you some other tax advantages, so check with the state in which you live. Also, 529 plans are offered by several low-cost providers, such as Vanguard or Fidelity. Check around to find the plan that makes the most sense for you. Review costs of the plan and the number of options provided because they are limited.

If your kids receive birthday money or special occasion money, have them put a portion of it right into their 529 plan. This is a great way to introduce the idea of investment to your kids. Relatives, such as grandparents, can even put money in the 529 if they want to gift any money to their grandchildren.

Chapter 20

Protecting Your Money

One year during my annual physical, the doctor reviewed my blood work results and said to me, "The bad news is you are going to die. The good news is it probably won't be today." After that, I got a new doctor. Not to be overly morbid, but he did have a point. Everybody is going to die someday. Planning for the inevitable is important, so make sure you are doing a few simple things to ensure your money is safe and is passed along according to your wishes after your ultimate demise. If you don't follow these simple steps, your family could be left financially vulnerable, and your hard-earned money left up for grabs or reduced by taxes or fees.

Beneficiaries

A designated beneficiary is a person or persons who will receive your money in case you die. Every financial account you own should have a designated beneficiary. These can include bank accounts, life insurance policies, retirement accounts, taxable accounts, money markets, and certificates of deposit.

Make sure when you are creating any of your financial accounts or buying a life insurance policy you provide beneficiary information right then.

When you designate a beneficiary, you typically can show a primary and secondary beneficiary. A primary beneficiary can be a single person, or several people that get a certain percentage of your money. For example, you could say you want fifty percent split between your father and mother, or 75 percent to your sister and 25 percent to your second cousin twice removed, or a hundred percent to your significant other.

If you die and none of the primary beneficiaries are alive, then the money will be distributed to the secondary beneficiaries you designate. Therefore, it is important to provide accurate and detailed information initially, and then review it on a regular basis as your family changes. If you ever are unfortunate enough to get a divorce, you may not want your ex-spouse as a beneficiary on your accounts.

Wills

A will is a legal document where you provide details about how you want to distribute your wealth and who will care for your minor children after you die. Wills are important for anyone, but they are critical if you have children.

Wills are also the place to detail any preferences for funeral services, where you want to be buried, and who should get important possessions in your life. I know both of my children are anxiously waiting to learn which of them will receive my basketball signed by NBA great Jeff Hornacek and my large collection of Iowa State Cyclone football helmets when I die. They will just have to wait until my will is read to get the great news!

I know this may hurt your feelings, but your kids probably won't care as much about your stuff as you do. I saw an incredibly funny cartoon where an elderly father and his son were standing in front of the father's garage. The garage door was open, and the inside of the garage was jam packed full of boxes and family "memorabilia" (aka junk). The father stood next to his son and proudly announced, "One day, Son, all of this will be yours."

When my mother died, she had not prepared anything detailing how she wished her possessions to be handed out amongst her five kids. I felt a lot like that kid in the cartoon. My mom didn't have much in the way of financially valuable possessions, but there were many emotionally valuable ones. You never know which of your things are meaningful to your kids or loved ones, so it is important to detail your wishes in writing. The distribution of my mother's things caused quite a bit of discomfort, angst, and lifelong hard feelings between my siblings. Kids handle the loss of their parents in different ways, and many times conflict between siblings is a result. Siblings may fight over possessions that have sentimental value at the same time they are dealing with their loss. Save your family members some grief, and detail where you want things to go in case more than one family member wants the same possession.

Money Decree
You are in charge of protecting your money, because no one else will.

It would also be easy to take the stance of not caring about what happens after you die, because, well, you're dead. The death of a parent, no matter at what age, is an emotional experience. Do your family a favor and provide details about how you want your estate to be handled when you are gone. However, the greater amount of assets you accumulate, the more important it is for you to be specific about how to handle those assets after you die. Many times, money changes people and can cause rifts within families no matter the situation. At least make it easier on them by providing specifics in your will.

Trusts

A **will** gives you the ability to detail how you want your affairs handled and your wealth distributed. **Trusts** give you the ability to transfer wealth in a more efficient manner. Without a trust, a transition of wealth may require probate, which is using the court system to legally transfer assets. This can be time-consuming and very costly. Also, by using the court system, the entire process is public to anyone who is interested. And the court decides the fair way to distribute your assets, which may be different than you want.

Basically, by utilizing a trust, you move the ownership of your key assets to the trust. While you are alive, the assets are still controlled by you. After you die, the assets are transferred according to the details of the trust.

Trusts are certainly more complicated and expensive to create compared to a will, but both are important for protection of your assets. Find a qualified estate attorney to provide you details and create the required documents to put your will and trust in place. It is also important to review the documents every few years or when you have a significant life change such as a marriage, divorce, birth of a child, or with a significant change in your finances.

Power of Attorney

Usually within your will and trust documents you should also have a power of attorney. The power of attorney provides guidelines for when you are still alive but are not able to make decisions about your estate. Work closely with an attorney about what this means to you and pick someone you trust. Providing a power of attorney to someone else gives them the ability to make decisions about your estate as if they were you.

PART IV

SPENDING MONEY (OR NOT)

Part IV: Spending Money (Or Not)

In Part I we learned about the importance of money. In Part II we learned about making money. In Part III we learned about saving money. Now comes the hard part – not spending more than you earn and making goals for saving.

This is the easiest place to derail your money train. It is so easy to spend. Businesses want you to spend money with them, so they will make it easy on you and even toy with your emotions through advertisements and marketing.

You can rack up charges on your credit cards without a plan to pay. The credit card company will not stop you until you hit your credit limit.

You can buy a brand-new car on credit based on several factors that may or may not actually show whether you can reasonably make the payments.

You can qualify for a home loan that is based on percentages of income, not necessarily your ability to repay the loan without extreme hardship.

We are a country of materialism, impulse buying, competing with our neighbors for nicer things, and immediate satisfaction. And these daily decisions are driving many people further and further into debt without hope of a successful recovery or financial freedom.

I want to give you some hacks, hints, tips, and guidelines to push away the materialism and focus more on your needs and experiences. When I'm on my death bed, I guarantee you I will not regret that I did not buy the most expensive cell phone, the biggest house in the neighborhood, or the nicest cars. I hope I will be thinking about the experiences I had with my loved ones along the way.

Life is not a competition about how much crap you can buy and hoard. There once was a comedian named George Carlin who did a bit about how people just bought houses so they could go out and buy stuff to fill them. Then they go buy bigger houses so they can go out and fill them up with *more* stuff. It's a trap. We buy houses and feel obligated to fill them up with stuff. Then when those rooms are all filled up, we buy more stuff to fill up our garages, so we must park our cars outside. If we see an empty space in our homes, we feel like we need to buy something to fill in the space. The goal is to fill up every available space in our lives with more stuff. Some things we need, some we don't.

Money Decree
Building wealth is not a competition.

I remember when my wife and I bought our current home as we planned to start a family. Although it is a modest home for the neighborhood, it was larger than our previous house. In fact, we went months having a living room with nothing in it because we didn't have enough furnishings from the old house to fill the new house. We were disciplined enough to know that we didn't need to buy furniture for it right away. It did look odd, and it drove my mother crazy. After her visits with us, she would tell my siblings how uncomfortable it made her to see a room with absolutely nothing in it.

Many years later, my wife went through a phase after reading a book about having too much stuff. She would look at an item in our house and ask herself if it brought her joy. If it didn't, it was kicked to the curb. We donated a lot of things during that phase. I am just thankful I got to stay.

With that said, it is ok to have stuff. But control how much you buy and how much you buy it for. Everyone has bills to pay for their needs. Remember our needs are shelter, food, and clothing. A multitude of other needs could include transportation to and from work, insurance, a cell phone, and internet capabilities. The focus here is to use techniques to buy what you need, along with what you truly enjoy, and not overspend on either. We must also constantly remind ourselves of the difference between wants and needs. We get into trouble when we think wants are needs, just because we want them badly.

Part IV: Spending Money (Or Not)

The chapters in this section provide lessons I have personally learned over time. I share them with the hope that you can use them in your life to control expenses and move up the Financial Pyramid.

Chapter 21

Find A Money Management Program

There is an old saying in business: "If you cannot measure it, you cannot manage it." This translates to our personal lives, also. To effectively manage your money and all your spending, you must first measure it. The measurement should be done in two ways. First, create a budget. Second, track every single dollar you make and spend. The best way to do this is through a money management software program. There is a plethora of free options out there that include just a plain old spreadsheet. Find one that works for you and stick with it. Just be sure that the program you choose can do at least these things:

- Create a detailed budget for all your income, spending, and saving.
- Enter every single financial transaction you complete in an easy way.
- Track the difference between your actual financial transactions and your budget.
- Observe all transactions made for several accounts, such as your checking account and savings accounts.

If the program can also provide a reminder for upcoming bills and an analysis of your cash flow, that would be even better. Having a visual overview of your upcoming bills and how it will impact your checking account can help you plan and not be surprised by a shortfall of cash.

Money Decree
Budget and track every single dollar you make and spend.

The program we have used for years is Microsoft Money and I would highly recommend it. It can be clunky at times, but it provides as much detail as you could ever want, and it is easy to use. Research different products and pick whichever one works for you, but don't pay for one. There are too many good free options available to you.

One of the first things many money management apps or programs will ask you to do is link your bank account with the app. By linking your bank account(s) with the app, all your transactions can be downloaded directly to the app automatically. This can certainly save time and hassle, but I highly recommend you do **not** link them for a couple of reasons. First is security. If you link your bank account, you are supplying an app (and the company that owns it) with information on how to gain entry to your bank account. This will include direct access to your hard-earned money and details about what you purchase and when. No one should ever have your bank account user ID and password unless they are someone you want to have direct access to your money. Additionally, if there is a security issue through the app and your money is stolen, the bank may not help you with any type of insurance since you knowingly provided your user ID and password to complete strangers.

The second reason to not link your financial app with your bank account is because there is value to manually entering transactions into your program. We will discuss this later in the book when we talk about reconciling your bank statements (please contain your excitement and do not look ahead), but if you automatically dump transactions made through your bank into your app, then you may not readily see transactions made in error, theft, or recurring transactions that need to be canceled. And I think there is value in requiring you to do the work on your own – an emotional value. If you must type in every single transaction you make, it will draw attention to how many transactions you're making and how much you're spending. When you must type in forty-five transactions from your local coffee shop, it may raise the issue about your caffeine spending problem.

The concept here is to use a software program as a tool to help you understand your money. You develop a plan of how you will spend your money (budget), and then you will track every single penny you spend so you can compare it to your budget. The program will help you understand where you overspend and how you can save more.

Just like any other tool you use, it is important you use it correctly to get the full benefit. Do you use the claw side of a hammer to pound a nail? No, that would be using the tool wrong and is just plain silly. Are you supposed to stand on the very top step of a ladder? No, that would be using the tool wrong and is unsafe.

Spend the time to find a money management tool you will use and commit time to use it. This is a critical step to understand and manage your spending – and move up the Financial Pyramid.

Chapter 22

Create A Budget
It's a Pain, But Do It Anyway

Now that you have found a software program to use, the next step is to create a budget for your income, spending, and saving. Start your budget process by grabbing a sheet of paper or opening a spreadsheet, such as Microsoft Excel. Create three columns. Down the left-hand column on the page, make a list of categories for your income, expenses, and savings. Think of the categories as buckets of money. You should be able to look in each bucket and easily tell how much you made, spent, or saved within that bucket and whether you should have made, spent, or saved more or less than you did.

The key here is to create an extensive enough list of buckets so all your money fits into one of those buckets, the more detailed the better. When completed, you should be able to know, with little or no effort, where all your money went. If you have a budget that has two buckets, one for your rent payment and one labeled "miscellaneous," then you're defeating the purpose. Each bucket should be self-explanatory and in the end be able to tell you the amount you made, spent, or saved for each bucket.

To help start this process, below you will see some examples for your money buckets.

MONEY BUCKET	6 Month Total	Monthly Average
Job Take Home Pay		
Side Hustle Income		
TOTAL INCOME		
Rent/Mortgage payment		
Food		
Clothing		
Uh oh fund		
Other savings fund		
Taxable retirement savings		
Car payment		
Car insurance		
Car gasoline		
Car registration		
Cell phone (Cost of phone)		
Cell phone plan (Cost of plan)		
Television subscriptions (Netflix, Apple TV, etc.)		
Electric bill		
Water/sewer bill		
Internet subscription		
Dining out		
Donations		
Entertainment		
Hobbies		
Healthcare (Doctor, Prescriptions, etc.)		
Home maintenance		
Life insurance		
Homeowners/Renters insurance		
Travel/Vacation		
TOTAL EXPENSES		
INCOME LESS EXPENSES		

The buckets above are similar to the ones we have been using for years, except we go into more detail for certain expenses. For example, because we like to travel a lot, our budget shows buckets within the travel category that include airfare, local transportation, lodging, meals, and admissions. This allows us to track specifically how we did for each bucket compared to our budget. Many of the above categories can be broken down further if you choose. The goal is to establish a budget and spending plan that is easily tracked for you. The only way to accomplish that is to establish a strong list of buckets.

From year to year, buckets can change. For example, the buckets for our kids have expanded over time to track things like how much we spend on their clothes, after school activities, sports teams, and school tuition.

The next step is to research every single dollar you have spent and saved over the last six months. Pull your credit card statements and bank statements to help you identify every single dollar made, spent, and saved. Put each transaction in one of the buckets and write the six-month total for each bucket in the center column marked "6 Month Total." As you review your transactions, you may find that you forgot a bucket. Just go ahead and create a new bucket and add it to your list. Ideally, you should be able to account for every dollar you spent and saved from your income.

Now, take a good hard look at your list. Any surprises about where your money went over the last six months? Was it hard to account for a portion of your hard-earned dollars? That's ok. That is part of the process – the realization of where your money is spent, even if that means you have no clue at this point.

The next step is to divide each bucket total by six, so you get an average monthly cost for each bucket. Some buckets, such as the car payments or television subscriptions, will be the same each month, but others, like your electric bill or dining out, will vary from month to month. By looking at a total over six months and dividing them out, it should give you a good perspective on how much you spend each month on average. Put the monthly numbers in the column on the right with the title "Monthly Average." Total both columns at the bottom of the page under the section "Total Expenses."

In this exercise, the savings totals are combined with your expense category since you are "spending" money on yourself by setting it aside for savings. It's helpful to consider your savings just like a bill. You have a deadline to pay it, and you should never miss a payment.

The last step is to calculate your income over this same time frame. Figure out your income over a six-month period and a monthly average, then enter them at the very top of the columns you created.

Now it is time for an eye-opening observation. Compare the top line marked "Total Income" with the bottom line marked "Total Expenses." If the top line is bigger than the bottom line, congratulations! Put more money in savings. If your bottom line is bigger than your top line, then as Ricky Ricardo would say, "You got some 'splaining to do!" If you have no idea what I am referencing, Google "I Love Lucy."

If your expense line is bigger than your income line, then you have some work to do. You are spending more money than you make, and something needs to give. This is a point where you need to get real with yourself and find which expenses need to be reduced or removed altogether. Notice I did not mention income. It is easy to say you need to make more money to cover your expenses, but that is not the easiest thing to do, or everyone would do it. As I'm sure you have been told, "Money does not grow on trees."

Remember earlier when we discussed that your goal for saving should be twenty percent of your income? Let's take a quick look and see how you're doing versus your goal. First, total the amount you put into all your savings accounts over the last six months that you just identified above. Secondly, take that number and divide by your total income for that same time frame. The income number you use should be your gross pay, not your take home pay. Take that number and multiply it by one hundred to give you the percent of income you are saving in after tax savings accounts. Add that percent to the pre-tax savings accounts, like your 401k. What is your overall level of saving? Is it at or above the goal of twenty percent? If not, you should identify ways to lower expenses and defer more money into your savings accounts.

If you are currently employed and not living within your means, then you have an expense problem. Expense problems can be hard to fix because they can be emotional and blind your better judgement. Overspending is easy to start, and hard to stop. People become accustomed to a certain standard of living, and it's tough to take some of those expenses away.

One of my favorite movie lines is from a movie called "A League of Their Own." It's about a women's professional baseball league created during World War II that took the place of the men's professional teams while many of the men were fighting in the war. The best player in the league was frustrated and talking to her manager about quitting the league because "it is too hard." His response was, "It's supposed to be hard. If it wasn't hard, everyone would do it. The hard is what makes it great."

Moving up the Financial Pyramid is hard. And it should be. If accomplishing your dreams were easy, you wouldn't find as much satisfaction in the accomplishment.

Knowledge Drop

The All-American Girls Professional Baseball League portrayed in "A League of Their Own" existed from 1943 to 1954. Over 600 women played in the league which consisted of 10 teams.

Much of the rest of this book will provide tips, techniques, and hacks on how to reduce or eliminate some of your expenses. But all the advice and guidance in the world means nothing without action from you. This is hard work, but the hard is what makes it great.

You have all the numbers in front of you to build a good budget. Now that you know how much you spend, you need to ask yourself how much you *should* spend to meet your goals. That becomes your budget to work to achieve. Establish reasonable spending for each of the categories *and* meet your savings goals. That means you must spend less than you make and save all the rest, which should be at least twenty percent of your income.

Now open your money management software app to enter all the information from the exercise above. Create your money buckets and enter the budgeted amount for each bucket based on your goals.

Congratulations! You now have a software program with a plan for monthly spending to move you forward toward financial stability. Take a moment to celebrate – but do it without spending money.

From this day forward, you should enter every financial transaction into your money app. As you begin entering all the transactions that track your spending, you should review your budget versus your actual spending at least once a month. Your software program makes it easy. It will build a report that should show your plan (budget) for each money bucket versus how much you spent from that bucket. Look at each line to see where you did well and where you have a leaky bucket.

Chapter 23

Recurring Payments Are the Devil

Now that you have a money management software program and a budgeting plan, the next step is to start tracking what you are spending in reality. From this day forward, every financial transaction you complete should be entered in your software program. You charged $37.50 from Old Navy on your credit card – enter it. You bought potato chips for $3.17 at the gas station with your debit card – enter it. You used $12.99 in cash for an extra-large nonfat vanilla caramel latte, extra hot with almond milk foam and cinnamon sprinkles at your favorite coffee shop – enter it. And make your life less complicated by ordering just a simple cup of coffee once in a while. Better yet, make one at home.

Typically, I will keep receipts for every transaction and put them in a pile on my desk before entering them into our software program every two or three days. If you can continually keep up with entering your receipts, the time it takes is small. If you wait too long or only enter them once a month, you will dread this task.

Within your money software program, you will create separate accounts for your checking account, savings accounts, and each credit card you possess. You can also add other savings accounts like money markets if you wish. Each transaction will be entered into the financial account you used for the purchase and dropped into the appropriate money bucket for tracking purposes compared to your budget.

Your software program should also help you manage transactions that happen automatically and where you may not get a receipt. These can include things like memberships in a gym, massage clubs, television streaming, cell phones, Costco, and Amazon. They can also include your mortgage or rent payments, HOA fees, and utility bills.

If you have any recurring payments, they can be entered into your software program to alert you of the upcoming bill and how much you anticipate it should cost. For example, if you have Netflix, you can set up a recurring payment to Netflix in your software program which will remind you that the payment is about to hit your checking account or credit card for the subscription price at the same time each month.

Recurring payments are a slippery slope. The great thing is they are automatic. The bad thing is they are automatic. Businesses *love* recurring payments. When you sign up for a service or membership with recurring fees, you generally link them to your credit card or checking account. The business gets paid automatically without having to send an invoice or remind you. They don't have to worry about whether you remembered to send them a check. They get paid automatically. If the price increases? They just increase the automatic payment they already have linked to your account. It is easy for them and easy for you.

However, recurring payments are too easy. Many people sign up for memberships or services and then never pay attention to the money coming out of their account. If you don't watch over these recurring charges, two things could happen. First, you could pay for services you don't use any longer. Second, you could end up overpaying for services because the businesses are banking (haha) on the fact that you don't look at their increased charges over time.

Think about that great gym membership you signed up for as a New Year's Resolution. You promised to go every single day and it was a good deal. The introductory offer was only $5.99 per month for the first six months. Well, six months later when you forgot you had the membership (as well as your resolution) and the introductory offer is done, the price went up to $25 per month. You are now paying $300 per year for something you don't even use – unless you watch your recurring charges. I'm not saying to forego a gym membership if it is financially viable for you, and it gets used. I am saying to watch out for recurring charges in your expenses.

Every business increases their rates. The question is whether the increases are reasonable *and* you still use and value the service they offer. The only way you know is if you track those expenses and make sure to scrutinize recurring charges, or you will have money escaping your bank account for no reason whatsoever.

Knowledge Drop

According to numerous studies, including one from the USA Today, up to 67% of gym memberships go unused and 7.4% only go once per month.

There are several effective ways to watch over any automatic recurring charges. First, as soon as you sign up for a recurring charge, enter it into your software program so you can see it pop up as a reminder whenever it is due. This will cause you to look at the charge and substantiate whether it's worthwhile.

Secondly, watch for price increases. Match your actual charge with the recurring charge in your software program to ensure you don't miss an unexpected or unreasonable price increase. Good examples of this can be found with satellite TV, streaming TV, internet services, or car insurance. They are well known for increasing charges at an unreasonable rate with little or no notice.

Thirdly, reconcile your statements every single month. Reconciling your statements means you compare the transactions you entered into your software program with the account statements of actual charges. When done properly, reconciling will immediately notify you of differences between your money program and the statement so you can question as to why. Did you forget to enter a transaction which would cause an inaccurate budget? Is there a change in pricing of a recurring charge? Was there an unauthorized charge?

Each month, your bank and credit card companies will produce statements showing all your transactions for the previous month. Take that statement and compare it with your money software program. Once you get good at it, this process should take no more than fifteen minutes per month. Your software program will have a reconcile button for each account you have. Go through that process to compare what your statement says versus what you have entered in the software program.

Why reconcile your bank and credit card statements?

1. The process will ensure you have accounted for every transaction during the month, so you know how much money you are spending from each money bucket.
2. It helps you monitor recurring charges to see price increases and cancel any products you no longer use.
3. It will alert you to fraud. Does your statement show charges that are unknown to you, or where you were charged more than your receipt shows?

Just recently, my family and I went out for dinner together. In the following days, I entered the cost of the meal in our software program based on the receipt we received from the restaurant. When it came time to reconcile my statement later in the month, I found that the restaurant had charged us twice for the meal. One charge was for the meal and the second was for the meal ***and*** tip. If I had not reconciled the statement, I may have missed the extra charge and paid out money for no reason whatsoever.

Accounting for every dollar you spend shows respect for the money you make and spend. That respect for your money will help you move up the Financial Pyramid. I understand that reconciling your statements is not fun and is tedious, but it is important. I enjoy reconciling our statements, but I'm weird.

Chapter 24

Insurance Gives You Assurance

The first time I bought insurance I got ripped off. My father and I were sitting in a banker's office getting a loan for a brand-new car (more on this story later), and the banker sold us on the idea to buy life insurance for the loan. The concept was that I would pay a little extra on my car loan toward an insurance policy and the loan would be forgiven if I died prematurely. The concept is great, and we bought off on the idea because my dad really trusted the banker. The reality is we could have purchased an insurance policy somewhere else that would have accomplished the same purpose, and a lot more, for a lot cheaper.

Everyone needs insurance of some kind. When you buy insurance, you pay a company some amount of money just in case something bad happens – a hospital visit, a car accident, a house fire. The company, in return, ensures they will pay for a portion of your hospital visit, car repairs, or home rebuilding. You pay for insurance, hoping you never have to use it. The same is true for the insurance companies because that's how they make money. They charge you a rate for the insurance, called a premium, in hopes you never file a claim (a request for money to compensate for a loss) and use the insurance policy. If you file a claim against your car or home insurance policy, your next policy may be at a higher rate. If you routinely file claims, or claims total more than you paid in premiums, your premiums will go up, or in the worst-case scenario, they will not insure you at all. Just know that insurance companies are a for-profit business, like any other.

Like other products and services sold in the world, you must do your homework before you buy insurance. First you must ensure you need the insurance, and secondly you get it at a fair price and terms. Here are a list of insurances starting with the ones you *absolutely* need, followed by types you *may* need:

Health Insurance

Why you *absolutely* need it: This protects you and your family in case you get sick. Guess what? No one expects to get sick. Especially when you are young, you may think you're invincible and health insurance is a second thought. Get it anyway. Nothing can damage your financial life quicker than a health issue. When you have a family, it is even more important because you are not just concerned about your own health, but that of your partner and children.

How to get it: The primary and most cost-effective way to get health insurance is through your employer. As we discussed in the "Making Money" section of the book, health insurance is a crucial benefit from an employer. When you sign up for health insurance through your employer, they will automatically take your portion of the health insurance premiums out of your pay checks. If you are not employed, or your employer does not offer health insurance, you can purchase it on the open market or a federal or state health exchange. In these cases, the health insurance offering may be very expensive, and the coverage will not be as extensive.

Other things to know: Ever wonder why health insurance is always a hot topic in politics and during our elections? Because health insurance is big business in the United States and there are pieces that are broken.

Health insurance companies, doctor's offices, laboratories, and pharmaceutical companies all want to make money. It is okay for businesses to make money because that is how they grow and thrive. However, issues can exist when unscrupulous business tactics are used by overcharging, sending unknowing patients unexpected bills, or insurance providers not wanting to cover a particular claim. And sometimes you get caught in the middle between what your insurance will pay for and what is being charged for the product or service you received. You will be responsible for the difference.

I cannot think of an industry where you buy a product or service and have no earthly idea how much it will cost you, but that is what happens within our healthcare system.

Please know that whatever insurance plan you choose, there is always an obligation upon you. Do not ever expect to walk into a doctor's office and receive services without a bill being sent to you. Your responsibility is to talk with your doctor, lab, pharmacy, and hospital about your healthcare to make sure you know the expectations and take full advantage of your insurance.

> **Knowledge Drop**
>
> Insurance policies can be purchased for body parts and various weird scenarios. According to the US Insurance Agents, more than $10 million dollars in alien abduction insurance has been written, with higher payouts available for people who are abducted frequently.

Here are some ways to mitigate your health care expenses beyond your premiums:

- Most health insurance covers an annual physical. Upon setting up an appointment for your physical, communicate clearly to the doctor's office the purpose of your visit so they do not charge you for something outside of the scope of an annual physical, unless additional tests are needed due to specific health concerns. You are there for an annual physical and whatever is covered fully by your insurance company. Many doctor's offices will try and upcharge you with products or services outside the scope of your physical, and you will be left holding the bill. Unfortunately, they usually do not tell you there are extra charges associated with these additional services. If you need additional tests, get them. Just understand they may not be free, and you should know and anticipate charges for those services.

- If you must complete blood work or get a special test such as an MRI or X-ray, talk with your doctor about the most cost-effective ways to complete these tests. Then, attempt to get the anticipated costs for these tests from the provider.
- When your doctor prescribes medicine, ask for a generic brand name when available because they will be significantly cheaper than name brand medicines and most times will provide the same results. Also, shop around for the best pricing on your medications because they can vary considerably among pharmacies. We started using a free service called GoodRx as a resource to identify the most cost-effective pricing of medications.
- Only use your doctor when needed. Do not go for issues you can resolve on your own, such as a cold, minor flu symptoms, or minor injuries.
- In non-emergency situations where you need to see a physician quickly, use urgent cares instead of the emergency room. The cost of the visit and your ultimate bill will be significantly less. Most insurance plans encourage you to utilize urgent cares versus emergency rooms because it will save both of you a significant amount of money.

Health insurance can be confusing and intimidating. Employers may provide you different plan options to choose from and it is easy to just pick the plan with the cheapest premium. As long as you know what you are getting for the money, that is fine. But if you pick the cheapest plan, expect to pay a greater share of the expenses when you visit your doctor.

Here are some key areas to pay attention to when reviewing a health insurance policy:

- **Co-payment:** This is an amount of money you must pay for an office visit with your primary doctor or specialist. Typically, these amounts will be printed on the insurance card you receive after you sign up for the health insurance. Know your co-payments.
- **Deductible:** This is an amount of money you must pay before your insurance company will start helping you pay health related bills. Deductibles are based on an annual basis. Know the amount of your deductible.
- **High deductible health plan:** To help keep health insurance premiums low, some insurance plans offer a high deductible, which requires you to pay more money before your insurance company starts pitching in. Typically, these types of plans are accompanied with a Health Savings Account and have cheaper premiums.
- **Health Savings Account (HSA):** This account allows you to contribute pre-tax money to use for future medical expenses. These are becoming more common because deductibles (and therefore out of pocket expenses) have increased dramatically with most health insurance plans. The HSA gives you a way to save pre-tax money to compensate for the higher deductible.
- **Co-insurance:** In a year's time, if you have met your required deductible amount, co-insurance kicks in. This is the amount you still need to pay after you exceed your deductible.
- **Out of Pocket Maximum:** The amount a policyholder must spend on eligible healthcare expenses through copays, coinsurance, or deductibles before the insurance starts covering all expenses.

Car Insurance

Why you *absolutely* need it: If you own a car, you need car insurance. It is not only required by law, but it protects you against a substantial loss related to a car accident.

How to get it: You can easily find car insurance quotes online or from insurance agents. Pick a name brand insurance company and get quotes from at least three or more. Make sure the quotes you receive have the same number of coverages so you have a good comparison for the price.

Other things to know: Car insurance policies generally last for a period of six months. You can be charged premiums monthly, but there will probably be an upcharge for the convenience. You can choose the size of your deductible with most policies. The higher deductible you choose, the lower your premiums. Don't choose a policy with a $5,000 deductible just because the premiums are cheaper. Whatever deductible you choose, you should be prepared to pay it. Make sure your uh-oh fund can easily cover any deductible costs. Accidents are called accidents for a reason, because they are never planned.

Requote policies every year to ensure you are getting the best deal because car insurance can vary wildly year to year even if you did not file a claim.

Homeowner's/Renter's Insurance

Why you *absolutely* need it: This insurance protects your house or apartment and its contents in case of damage or complete loss. When you buy a home, it is generally the largest investment you have. Protect it. If you live in an apartment, it is always a good idea to protect all your belongings in case your neighbor accidentally sets the building on fire while doing a science experiment with a Bunsen burner.

How to get it: Most of the name brand insurance companies that provide car insurance also provide homeowners/renters insurance. Many times, if you buy the car and home policies from the same company, you will receive a discount.

Other things to know: When you buy a home, your mortgage company may require you to have insurance. They will add the cost of your insurance to the monthly payment to the mortgage company to ensure the policy remains in place. Typical policies are annual, but they can be billed monthly for a surcharge. Requote policies every year to ensure you are getting the best deal.

Life Insurance

Why you *may* need it: Bear with me while we wander into uncomfortable, yet important, territory. I know you are going to live a long and happy life, but insurance causes us to plan for all the things we really do not want to happen. The reality is people die. Feel free to take a moment to compose yourself due to this reality.

People purchase life insurance policies for themselves to take care of their loved ones once they die. The purpose is to provide them money to cover unpaid debts, funeral costs, and supplement lost income since you will no longer be there to provide.

> **Knowledge Drop**
>
> The longest human lifespan is that of Jeanne Calment of France (1875–1997), who lived to age 122 years and 164 days. The United Nations estimate a global average life expectancy of 72.6 years for 2019 – the global average today is higher than in any country back in 1950.

The math here is relatively simple, although morbid. Pretend you die. Look beyond the emotional impact of us missing you and make a list of what financial impacts that will leave on your loved ones. If you are young with no family or debts, then life insurance may not make much sense. However, if you have a family, a mortgage, car loans, and are the main provider of income, then life insurance is a must. You have others who depend on you for income and to help with expenses, so your loss will be detrimental financially.

At a minimum, you should get life insurance that pays off all your debts. Providing additional money to take the place of your lost income for a few years is even better.

How to get it: The great news is that if you are young and healthy a life insurance policy is relatively cheap. Shop around online and with some of the larger insurance brokers to give you some competitive quotes and insight on a term life insurance policy. A term life insurance policy will provide life insurance coverage for a specific time frame and a fixed monthly price for the entire term of the policy. Steer away from other policies that are not term life. They can be incredibly expensive, and the return is suspect.

Many employers provide small life insurance policies included in your benefits package. When you are young without a family or debt, that may be all you need.

Other things to know: If you get a term life insurance policy, make sure the term is long enough to take care of your debts, such as your mortgage, or else you will run the length of your term and have to buy a new insurance policy at a greater price because you are older and closer to your, ahem, demise.

Steer away from getting additional term life insurance through your employer. They are typically more expensive than what you can get on the open market.

Be careful with life insurance products. There are many products on the market, and they can be very complicated and confusing. You can easily be sold products you don't need, be misled about their benefits, or get overcharged. For example, not too long before my father died, my parents bought a new term life insurance policy that only paid out a portion of what it was supposed to the first few years it was in place. I am guessing it saved them some money, but it was not worthwhile because it did not cover the needed expenses after he passed away.

Short-term and Long-term Disability Insurance

Why you *may* need it: If you become hurt or disabled and cannot work to earn an income, short-term and long-term disability may help supplement your income. If you were to get the coronavirus and had to miss work for a few weeks, short-term disability insurance may help supplement your income. If you fall off a ladder while trimming your tree, causing you to break a leg that must be immobilized for two months, then a long-term policy may help you.

Short-term policies cover just a few weeks and long-term policies may cover a few months or more. Both will generally compensate you for a portion of regular pay under certain circumstances. If your uh-oh fund is securely in place, I would forego the short-term disability policy.

How to get it: Many employers provide competitively priced policies as a part of your benefits package. Read the fine print to understand when the policy starts, how long it lasts, and how much money it provides if you file a claim. Most disability policies provide a percentage of your income and will not pay all of what you were making for income.

Other things to know: As with life insurance policies, you must envision what would happen if you could not work for a period of time. Disability policies can help get you to the point where you can go back to work again.

Umbrella Insurance

Why you *may* need it: When you follow all my guidance in this book and become rich as hell, you should consider an umbrella policy to help further protect your assets. An umbrella policy, as its name portrays, covers all your assets for excess liability above and beyond what your car and homeowner's policies will cover. The umbrella policy can also provide you coverage for claims that may be excluded from other policies including false arrest, libel, or slander. Additionally, they can protect you from bodily injury liability and property damage liability claims. Talk with an insurance broker about your individual situation to ensure you understand your options for umbrella coverage.

How to get it: Because the umbrella policy goes hand in hand with your other policies, you generally need to get the umbrella policy, car policy, and homeowner's policy from the same company. There are exceptions, but it is best to approach a name brand insurance company or broker to help you find the best coverage for you.

Other things to know: Typically, umbrella insurance is offered in $1 million increments.

Travel Insurance

Why you *may* need it: In some rare cases, it may be worthwhile to purchase travel insurance to protect a pending vacation or other type of travel. This insurance may help protect you financially in case you bought nonrefundable travel and cannot go on the trip.

Beware! Most people see travel insurance and assume it will provide coverage for any reason. Read the fine print. In most cases, the travel insurance only helps you in very specific incidents. For example, it may provide you a credit voucher instead of a full refund. The policy may only give you a refund if there is a death of one of the travelers. If you have a close family member that passes away the day before you leave, you may be out of luck.

How to get it: The place you book the trip generally offers opportunities for travel insurance. This includes airlines and travel agencies. You can also purchase it on the open market, but only choose reputable, name brand companies. The open market often provides insurance coverage that can be cheaper and more extensive.

Other things to know: If you are working with a travel company that offers travel insurance, be sure to look at the name of the company that is selling you the insurance policy. If it is the travel agency itself, then beware. If the travel agency goes bankrupt and you lose all your reservations, then your insurance policy may be worthless, as well. The better scenario is to purchase a policy from an independent, reputable company that can provide you coverage in case there is an issue with the travel company.

Chapter 25

How to Get Credit for Good Credit

Throughout your life, you expect to get credit for things you do well. You work hard in school, and you expect a good grade along with positive praise from your teacher. At work, you come in early, stay late, and overachieve, then you expect acknowledgement from your boss, along with the occasional raise and promotion. You buy your wife those expensive chocolates she dearly loves so she will acknowledge her undying love for you and express her happiness that she chose you as her partner. All so you can sit and watch football all day long.

The same is true for your financial decisions. You want to be given credit for all the good financial decisions through your life. Beyond the fact that good financial decisions will provide you security and move you up the Financial Pyramid, certain financial decisions you make can give you other opportunities that directly impact your finances.

Your financial well-being is graded by several entities through a credit report and credit score associated with your name. The information detailed in your credit report and credit score are used by other companies and organizations to determine your financial wellness and security. Based on your performance, you may have the opportunity to receive a loan, cheaper interest rates, better insurance premiums, and even help you get a job.

Receiving loans or credit from institutions is incredibly important. Given the opportunity, credit will allow you to buy anything from new furniture to a new house. But credit is not given; it is earned. Financial institutions use your credit report and credit score as a basis of whether you are a reliable person to loan money to. If they decide you are, it's your responsibility to respect that institution by paying back every dollar you borrowed. So, let's focus in on how you get institutions to loan you money in the first place.

Credit Report

A credit report is similar to how a teacher details your coursework during a semester in school. They show you all the work you did on assignments, tests, and quizzes along with the grade for each.

Your credit report details your specific credit history by noting how you have done with each of your individual financial accounts, just like your assignments in school. The credit report will review details about your current open accounts, closed accounts up to ten years old, the amount of available credit on each account, and payment history.

Your credit history is managed by three credit bureaus: Equifax, Experian, and TransUnion. Every time you get a loan or credit card, the company you received the credit from provides details about your bill paying habits to one, two, or all three of the bureaus. Each company reports a bit differently, so it's not unusual they don't report information to all three bureaus. Also included on your credit report are accounts that were sent to collections for payment and bankruptcies.

If you stop paying back money you owe to a company, they will eventually send your account to collections. Collection companies are third party businesses who collect unpaid balances on behalf of the business you owe. Many times, these businesses can be ruthless and downright mean when trying to collect the money. Additionally, any accounts sent to collections can hurt your credit report for up to seven years. If you struggle to pay a bill, the best advice is to immediately and respectfully work with the company you owe and try to resolve it before it gets to the point of collections. Try to negotiate a reasonable agreement with them to repay the money. Once you come to an agreement, be sure to follow your commitment to them. After all, the company provided you a product or service and they deserve to be compensated. Most companies will work with you as long as you show you're trying to work with them.

The keys to a successful credit report are twofold: To have some credit available to report to the bureaus, and to pay your bills on time. Companies that loan money want to see you have had a successful track record in managing your finances. If you run into trouble and cannot make a payment on time, call the company immediately to discuss your situation and work with them to establish a solution to repay them in a timely manner. Don't ghost your creditors like you did your ex-girlfriend. Communicate with them *before* your bill is due by explaining your situation and your plan to pay them, along with the time frame to do so.

Knowledge Drop

According to a 2018 study published in Psychology Today, approximately 25 percent of men and women reported having been ghosted in a romantic relationship, and 22 percent admitted to having ghosted someone else.

Credit Score

If your credit report provides details similar to individual assignments in school, the credit score is equivalent to your GPA. The credit score is a number created to evaluate your credit worthiness. The larger your number, the better. Some businesses and lenders create credit scores unique to their needs based on information that is specifically relevant to them. A credit card company is focused on different details of your history than a mortgage company, for example.

The most widely produced credit score is through the Fair Isaac Corporation (FICO). The three bureaus produce FICO scores that range from 300 to 850, but they may differ from each other because they may show different pieces of your history.

Each reporting agency may be a bit different with their scoring, but here is an overview, according to Experian, about what each credit score means:

CREDIT SCORE	RATING
800 – 850	Exceptional
740 – 799	Very Good
670 – 739	Good
580 – 669	Fair
300 – 579	Poor

Your continued focus must be to maintain your FICO score at a *good* rating or better. This will provide you options for credit when you need it. If your FICO score gets into the *very good* and *exceptional* ranges, you will see a very positive impact on loan terms such as lower interest rates.

Your FICO score is made up of five factors:

1. **Payment History – 35% of your score.** This is the most important piece of your FICO score, so be sure to make your payments on time and remain in good standing with your accounts.

2. **Amount of Debt – 30% of your score.** This tracks the amount of money you owe compared to the size of available credit. This is called credit utilization. For example, if you have a credit card with a credit limit of $5,000 and you have a balance of $4,000, your utilization is eighty percent. Ideally, your credit utilization should be below thirty percent to help improve your FICO score. Companies do not want to see credit cards "maxed out" because this can show you are spending beyond your means.

3. **Credit History Length – 15% of your score.** The longer you have a revolving (or ongoing) account like a credit card,

the better. That doesn't mean you have to carry a balance month to month, only that you have an active card. This portion of the score is looking at the amount of time you have held on to an account as opposed to bouncing from one account to another. Many credit cards entice you with special deals where you can transfer balances between accounts. Do not get in the habit of transferring your balances around to different cards, trying to reduce interest rates or delay payments. Stick with a good card that meets your needs and pay off your balance every month.

4. **Amount of New Credit – 10% of your score.** Your score can be impacted if you open several new accounts all at the same time. This could show a risk to a creditor because you are potentially increasing the amount of your overall debt, so it will negatively impact your FICO score.

5. **Credit Mix – 10% of your score.** Your FICO score can improve if you have varying types of accounts like credit cards, retail accounts, car loans, and mortgages.

Other Things to Know

Because of its importance, make sure your credit report is and remains accurate by checking it annually. You can check your credit history for free one time per year, per bureau and any time you were recently denied credit from a lender. You can check one bureau every four months or check all of them at the same time each year. My preference is to space them out every four months in case there is an issue you need to dispute with a credit bureau. Just put a reminder in your calendar so you don't forget.

The best place to check your credit report is through www.annualcreditreport.com. Just know that the annual service is free, and you should not have to give your credit card information. Many of the bureaus will try to sell you upgrades and additional services that I have not found necessary. They will provide you details about your credit report, but not your credit score. Most credit card companies and some banks now offer regular updates on your credit score with no additional charge to you.

Since identity theft and credit fraud has become more prevalent in the world, keep a close eye on your credit history to make sure it's accurate. The three bureaus also allow you to put a credit freeze on each account for some added security. A credit freeze stops all outside entities from getting access to your credit report or opening any new accounts. You can temporarily lift the freezes by signing into each bureau's website if you are applying for credit somewhere. Again, this service is free to you. Do not get misled into paying to put a freeze on your credit accounts.

The Impact

A good credit history and good FICO score gives you an opportunity to get credit cards, buy a car, or a new house. A higher FICO score will get you better interest rates on loans and could even improve your insurance premiums. Many insurance companies have linked how you manage your finances to other areas in your life that reduce the amount of risk in filing insurance claims. Just like a teenage driver who gets a lower car insurance rate because of their grades, insurance companies give that same benefit to those with higher credit scores.

Additionally, employers may look at some facets of your credit history (with your approval) to evaluate how you manage your finances to help predict what kind of an employee you may be. The credit score certainly is not the only factor considered, but you do not want it to be a deal breaker if the company is evaluating more than one person for an open job. If you apply for a financial position within a company, expect a more detailed background check of your personal financial history. In this case, your financial management could be a significant consideration in getting a job. If you cannot manage your own finances very well, who is to say you will manage the company's finances any differently?

How to Improve your FICO Score

Immediately upon graduating from college and accepting my first real job, my dad and I went in search for a car. At the time, I was a proud owner of an old, yet reliable, Toyota Celica with over 100,000 miles and a manual moon roof. I was moving from Iowa to Arkansas to start my career and I knew an upgraded ride was an important step.

After finding a car to my liking, which was a 1992 charcoal gray Chevy Lumina (a real head-turner), we approached the local bank to apply for a loan. My dad and I sat in two uncomfortable chairs, in a cramped office across from a very serious lady with a large beehive hairdo sitting behind an oversized desk. My father was cosigning on my loan (more on this later), so I don't remember it being too hard to get the approval. She seemed pleasantly surprised by my modest (boring) choice for a car. As she read aloud the word "Lumina" on the piece of paper in front of her, she almost said it as a question – with her eyebrows raised and a slight squint. She might have had a smirk on her face. I felt like she was happy with my choice and recognized I was a highly intelligent person, and she was glad I was now part of the debt-paying society. Or it could have been she had never heard of such a dull car before.

Either way, she got the loan paperwork completed. As she set the documents in front of me, she handed me a pen, looked into my eyes with a hard, penetrating stare and said, "This is the most important loan of your life. Make these car payments on time – every time." I grabbed the pen with my shaking, sweaty right hand and said in a quivering voice, "Yes, ma'am."

She was right. And I did.

I paid my loan partly because it was the right thing to do and partly because I wanted a good credit score that I could use in the future. And partly because that lady scared the crap out of me. Whatever motivates you, I guess, just as long as you pay your bills on time – every time.

The best way to improve your FICO score is to have an excellent credit report. That is done by establishing credit and making payments on time, every time. Remember that financial institutions want to see a credit history that includes paying your bills when they are due. The easiest way to achieve this history is through a credit card because they are reasonably easy to obtain.

In your late teenage years, find yourself a no-fee credit card and use it a few times a month. This is the important part: pay it off every month. We will discuss credit cards more later, but for now just know that credit cards should never be used for purchases unless you plan to pay them off completely when your credit card bill is due each month.

A credit card is the easiest and fastest way to establish a positive credit report and FICO score but it's also the easiest way to go into debt. If you have a plan and the discipline to pay off your bill every month, you'll be just fine. If you get a credit card with a limit of $500 and you immediately max out your card in an afternoon with purchases of Takis, Dutch Bros., and fake nails, then you have defeated the purpose. This is the first step in your goal of establishing an excellent credit rating that you can use in the future. At some point, you will need credit to buy a car or a house. Your first credit card can be the foundation to build upon to create an excellent credit report for your future.

Chapter 26

Make Debt a Good Four-Letter Word

Debt can be the nastiest four-letter word for many. Debt can be easy to get, and hard to shed. Debt can help you move up the Financial Pyramid or it can leave you broke. Debt can cause anxiety, stress, and regret. But if used effectively, debt can put you on the right financial track. In the ideal world, you pay cash for every single transaction you make, and you never have any debts. However, that is not always possible or viable, especially when buying more expensive things like cars or homes. The goal is to use debt only when you need to and under reasonable conditions.

Any time you borrow something from someone with the expectation to repay, you have a debt. Borrow a cup of sugar from your neighbor; it is a debt until you return the favor. Your friend buys the first round of happy hour drinks; it is a debt until you buy the second round. Your girlfriend throws you a lit rager for your thirtieth birthday; it is a debt until you throw a lit rager for her.

A financial debt is when you borrow money from someone with the promise and obligation to pay them back. Whether you make a charge on your credit card or get a loan from a bank, you have borrowed money with an obligation to repay it. We'll focus on credit cards in the next chapter, so let's dig deeper into bank loans here. A bank loan allows you to buy things you need or want, including furniture, a car, a house, or school tuition. Then you pay them back monthly until the loan is fully paid. The bank will charge you interest on the loan, which is their profit for loaning you the money.

Debt can be good if all of these apply:

- You are getting a loan based on an item that is a reasonable want or need.
- You do not have the cash to pay for the item outright.
- You pay for a portion of the purchase up front through a cash down payment.
- You have acceptable plans to pay off the loan on time or early.
- The loan is structured with terms that are reasonable and competitive.

If you are living paycheck to paycheck and you get a loan to buy a brand-new Mercedes SUV, the debt is bad. This is not a reasonable want or need and you do not have acceptable plans to repay the loan.

If you take out a loan for a family vacation to Disneyland Paris, but you have not met any of your savings goals, then this debt is not a reasonable want or need.

If you get a payday loan with thirty percent interest charges so you can bet on the Kentucky Derby, the loan is not a reasonable want or need and the terms of the loan are not reasonable or competitive.

Beyond the decision making about whether to get a loan, understanding how a loan works is incredibly important. Too many people will only focus on the size of their payment when deciding on a loan. By understanding all facets of a loan, you can save a lot of money, especially when you buy something expensive like a car or home. The relationship between the interest rate, size of the loan, length of the loan, and payment size should all be considered when taking out a loan.

So, let's pretend you are buying a newly launched cell phone for the retail price of $5,000. (This was just to get your attention and help you understand how a loan works. I do not condone or recommend ever buying the latest new phone, especially for $5,000.) To purchase the phone, you receive a loan at a five percent interest rate, and you must repay it within twelve months. Below is a visual of what your payments would look like. Do not be intimidated, overwhelmed, or simply shut down over the chart because it looks complex. We'll go over it step by step with the hope this information will become easy for you to understand if it is not already.

For you math geeks, the numbers in the chart are rounded up so they are easier to read and understand.

This chart is called an amortization schedule, which just shows the breakdown of each payment made for a loan.

Month	(A) Beginning Balance	(B) Total Payment	(C) Interest	(D) Principal	(E) New Balance
1	$5,000	$428	$21	$407	$4,593
2	$4,593	$428	$19	$409	$4,184
3	$4,184	$428	$17	$411	$3,773
4	$3,773	$428	$16	$412	$3,361
5	$3,361	$428	$14	$414	$2,947
6	$2,947	$428	$12	$416	$2,531
7	$2,531	$428	$11	$417	$2,114
8	$2,114	$428	$9	$419	$1,694
9	$1,694	$428	$7	$421	$1,273
10	$1,273	$428	$5	$423	$851
11	$851	$428	$4	$425	$426
12	$426	$428	$2	$426	$0
TOTALS		**$5,136**	**$136**	**$5,000**	

Column A is your balance before each payment is made starting with the original loan amount of $5,000.

To pay off the loan in twelve months, with an interest rate of five percent, your required payment is $428 per month. The monthly payment of $428 is under **Column B.**

Each payment is made up of two pieces: Interest in **Column C** and Principal in **Column D**. The principal is the amount you're paying of the original $5,000 on each payment and the interest is your charge to the bank for the loan (the bank's profit).

Interest is calculated as a percentage of the amount owed at the time of the payment, and the rate given is an annualized rate. If your interest rate is five percent, that means you'll pay a rate of five percent over a year's time. However, you generally make monthly payments, not annual payments on loans, credit cards, or anything else where interest charges apply. In our example, the interest rate is calculated by taking the amount owed each month, multiplied by the five percent interest and divided by twelve since you pay the loan monthly.

So, in month one, you make a payment of $428 with $21 of the payment going toward an interest charge ($5,000 x 5% = $250 / 12 = $21) and the rest toward reducing the loan amount (principal).

In **Column E** "New Balance" represents the updated principal balance after each loan payment. After month one, you paid $407 in principal, so you take $5,000 and subtract $407 which makes a new loan balance of $4,593. This becomes the new balance where interest charges are calculated. You can see this in Column C where your interest charges decrease each month.

> **Knowledge Drop**
>
> According to Wikipedia, the first commercial cell phone was priced at $3,995 in 1984, which equates to $9,952 in today's dollars. It looked a lot like holding a brick to your ear.

As an overview, you have a loan of $5,000 where you are paying twelve monthly payments for $428. That means you will pay a total $5,136 for that $5,000 phone. Not only did you overpay for a new phone at $5,000, but you paid an additional $136 to buy it.

Why is this important? First, it gives you a visual to see that you pay a lot more interest in the beginning part of a loan than you do at the end. Why? Because your principal is higher at the beginning, and that is where the interest (or finance) charges are calculated.

Secondly, knowing how a loan works in detail can save you a bunch of money. With this knowledge, you can intelligently change the length of the loan, negotiate interest rates, or modify the size of the loan to help manage your finances better.

Let's look at how tweaking the payment terms can impact how much a loan ultimately costs you.

Example 1: The interest rate increases from 5% to 7%

I want you to pretend that your BFF sees your new phone and gets so jealous they want one too. (Again, this is a story for illustration purposes only, and buying a phone just because someone else did is just plain stupid!) But your BFF did not buy this book and they do not understand loans as well as you. Their bank gave them a 7% interest rate compared to your 5%. Here is a chart comparing the difference. (Again, for you math geeks, the numbers are rounded up so they are easier to look at, so please don't email me saying my math is wrong.)

	Interest Rate	Monthly Payment	Total Interest	Total Paid
Your Phone	5%	$428	$136	$5,136
BFF Phone	7%	$433	$192	$5,192

By raising the interest rate on the $5,000 loan from five percent to seven percent, your BFF's monthly payment increased to $433 from your $428, or $5 higher per month (a twelve percent increase). Their total interest charges for the loan increased from $136 to $192 or by $56 (a whopping 41 percent increase).

What is the moral of this example? Negotiating and comparing loans offering lower interest rates may not seem like a big deal, but in the long run can save you a lot of money. And your BFF needs to read this book.

Example 2: The payment terms increase from 12 months to 18 months

In this example, you and your BFF are purchasing your overpriced phones at the exact same time and get the same interest rate of five percent. However, your BFF can't afford the phone, so they want to overcome this hurdle by lowering their monthly payments.

Tim, the phone sales guy with the mint green shirt, greasy hair, and creepy smile, is more than accommodating. He says he can certainly get your friend a lower payment, with no worries at all. How does he do it? He increases the length of the loan from twelve months to eighteen months. This lowers the payment from $428 to $289 per month. Pretty cool, huh? Before you thank Tim profusely for his hard work and dedication to his craft, let's look at the chart below to see what happened:

	Payments	Rate	Monthly Payment	Total Interest	Total Paid
Your Phone	12	5%	$428	$136	$5,136
BFF Phone	18	5%	$289	$200	$5,200

Well, your BFF accomplished their goal of reducing their payment from your $428 to $289 (a reduction of $139 or 32 percent). And Tim accomplished his goal, too. He just increased his commission because by increasing the loan to eighteen months, the total amount of interest paid to him increases from $136 to $200 (a $64 increase or 47 percent). You have now paid $5,200 for that $5,000 overpriced phone.

The interest charges increase considerably because you're holding onto the loan for a longer time, so it takes longer to reduce your principal balance. Instead of paying down your debt faster on a twelve-month loan, you are paying it off over eighteen months, allowing more time to rack up interest charges.

What is the moral of this example? Increasing a payment term may lower your payment, but it increases the amount of interest charged, the overall cost of the loan, and ultimately the overall cost of whatever you bought. And Tim needs a new shirt. And a haircut.

A common trap with loans is that you only focus on the payment. You can easily lose money by overlooking the other pieces of the loan, such as the interest rate and loan term. Ask questions of your lender and compare amortization schedules like the ones above to see the best scenario for you. Negotiate the interest rate and adjust the length of the loan.

Example 3: Make a down payment on your loan

In this example, let's look at how a down payment, or upfront payment, would impact your loan. Because you've worked so hard, you have set aside money from your paycheck each week to help pay for your overpriced phone. You have $500 in your savings account that will help fund the $5,000 phone. When you apply for the loan with the cell phone company, you can happily report that you will be making a $500 down payment on your purchase. This will reduce the amount you finance to $4,500 on your twelve-month loan with a five percent interest rate. Let's see if it makes a difference.

	Loan Amount	Monthly Payment	Total Interest	Total Paid
No Down Payment	$5,000	$428	$136	$5,136
$500 Down Payment	$4,500	$385	$123	$5,123

By putting $500 down, your payment decreases by $43 per month and the total interest you will pay on the loan decreases by $13 (almost ten percent less). Most loans you receive should include some sort of a down payment, especially for bigger purchases like a car or house. It requires you to save some money before you make a purchase and in turn it will lower your payment and overall cost of the loan.

The Low or No Interest Loan

As we discussed in the last chapter, your credit score can really impact your interest rate. People that have higher credit scores are deemed to be more reliable and more likely to pay back a loan, so they are given a lower interest rate because the bank sees them as a lower risk. In turn, someone who has a lower or poor credit score, may not be eligible for a loan or the loan will be at a higher rate because they are deemed at higher risk of not repaying the loan.

Those people who have great credit scores may also have an opportunity to receive low or no interest rate loans. To encourage you to buy their products, some companies will offer special promotions through the terms of a loan. This is often seen in the car buying industry, but in our younger years we also did this when buying furniture.

When we had a need for a chair, couch, or new bed, we waited for the local furniture store to run a sale for special financing. Typically, the special was something like a 24-month loan that was interest free for the first six months. We'd take out a loan on the furniture with the full intention of repaying within the six-month interest-free time frame. Pretty clever, huh?

These were great deals when we had the money to repay within the time limit because we picked up a loan for no additional cost. We just borrowed the furniture store's money for free. They run these specials to encourage sales, but they are also hoping you won't repay within the six-month time frame.

Even though we rarely need to do this anymore, these opportunities are available with many businesses.

Be careful with the terms of these types of loans. Some loans have "deferred interest," which means if you don't repay the loan within the special time frame (in this case six months), you'll be charged the interest from day one of the loan if you still have a balance past the introductory time frame. This totally defeats the purpose of taking advantage of the interest free loan, because then it is no longer interest free.

The same can be true for loans with low introductory rates that are jacked up to much higher rates later in the loan repayment. Be sure to read and understand the terms of the loan so you can take full advantage of the special offer. The company providing you the loan is hoping you buy from them due to the special offer, but really do not take advantage of that offer.

Another consideration is the price of the product you are buying. Do not go buy a couch for $200 above the competition just because they had a loan for free interest. Do the math and understand the overall cost, including interest charges.

What About Your Current Loans?

For the sake of argument, pretend that you have ignored your dad, or you were not really listening to him when he explained loans and debt. So now you're reading this book and understand that you need to control your debt. You currently have a car loan, credit card debt, and/or a student loan that needs to be paid off. Even though you are making payments on each, you want to start paying them off quicker with extra cash you have. Which one do you pay off first?

Look at the terms of each type of debt you have and make a priority list based on the interest rate you are being charged. The one with the highest interest rate is costing you the most money and should be paid down first. Typically, it always starts with the credit cards. Credit card debt is the easiest way to get into trouble by charging too much and it is also the type of credit that costs you the most. As we will discuss in the next chapter, a credit card can help you with a lot of things, but if you don't pay it off each month, you can get into financial trouble fast.

Chapter 27

Credit Cards are Not Loans

A few truths about credit cards: They are relatively easy to get, they make it incredibly easy to buy things, and they are a simple way to get yourself into spiraling debt.

Credit cards can be good – if, and only if, they are used properly. Credit cards are great only if they are used for purchases that have a purpose within your budget *and* you pay off your balance every single month.

Credit cards are an example of revolving credit. That means you are given a maximum amount you can spend on the account (called a credit limit), and you don't have to pay a fixed amount like you do with a car loan or mortgage. You can make purchases up to the credit limit and you are not necessarily required to pay off the entire balance each month. This is what can get you in significant trouble.

First of all, your credit limit should not be seen as a goal for how much you can spend! Spending up to your credit card limit will hurt your credit score as we discussed earlier, because ideally you have a balance that is no greater than thirty percent of your credit limit. Additionally, if you have spent your credit limit, there is a strong likelihood that you do not have the money to pay off the entire balance of your card.

Credit card companies want you to use their cards and not pay them off each month. In fact, they make more money if you don't.

Credit card companies make money in two primary ways. First, they charge you a high interest rate if you maintain a balance or when you use your card for cash advances. Second, they charge transaction fees to the businesses where you make your purchases. All of that is fine, because companies should be able to make money on the services they provide. However, that doesn't mean you should get sucked into a pit of debt by using your credit cards improperly.

A loan (or credit) is when you borrow money for some purpose and then pay it back over time with reasonable terms which includes a fair interest rate and timetable. The credit card has none of those characteristics.

It is way too easy to swipe your card and build up charges that cannot be repaid each month. Then, if you can't pay off your entire credit card bill that month, a large interest charge will be added to the next month's bill. If you aren't careful, your credit card debt will quickly climb to out-of-control levels.

Think of your credit card as an equivalent to cash, except better. The credit card is better, because it not only helps you build a credit score, but you don't have to handle paper money or coins – you just swipe. No worries about exact change or fumbling with germ infested bills while waiting at the lengthy In-n-Out drive thru. However, credit cards should be treated just like cash in that if you don't have the money to pay for the credit card charge, you shouldn't make the charge. Your credit card bill should be paid in full every single month.

Honestly, credit card companies want you to use their card and not pay the bill in full each month. An account that has a balance rolling over from month to

Knowledge Drop

Paper money can reportedly carry more germs than a household toilet. Viruses and bacteria can live on bills for up to 48 hours, and bills are often contaminated with cocaine residue.

month gives them an opportunity to charge you more and more interest. If you pay off your entire bill each month and you never use your card for a cash advance, you will never pay interest charges on your credit card.

Here is another secret about credit card companies – they really do not know what you can "afford," and they really do not care. It is your job to only buy what is within your budget and to pay off your bill each month.

Credit cards are big business. It seems like every industry is getting into the credit card business – airlines, retail stores, grocery stores, cell phone providers, and online stores, along with the traditional banks, that can provide cash back or travel awards. Credit cards are big business because companies can make a large amount of money off people who use the cards. According to Debt.org, which provides information about debt in America, the average credit card holder has at least four credit cards and each household has close to $8,400 in credit card debt.

Over your lifetime, you will be inundated with credit card offers. Be prudent with your credit card strategy and stay focused on paying off your credit card each month. The rest of this chapter will discuss other details about how credit cards work and provide you some ideas about credit card strategies.

Minimum Payments

Every month, you will receive a statement from your credit card company that shows your current balance and all the transactions you made during the month. Somewhere at the top of your statement, there will be a line that says, "Minimum Payment." This is a trick! Remember that credit card companies charge interest on any balance not paid off each month, so they want you to pay something less. Therefore, they have invented the "Minimum Payment." If you only make the minimum payment, you are only paying down a fraction of the overall balance you owe. Most credit card companies will make their minimum payment only one to three percent of the total balance on your card. If you only make a one percent payment of your balance, your credit card debt will quickly spiral out of control. Ignore the minimum payment and pay off your bill every month. If you get in a pinch, pay off something higher than the minimum payment reflected on your statement.

Annual Fees

Many credit cards have annual fees, and some are outrageous. Until you become an expert at using (and paying off) your credit card and establishing a credit card strategy, there is no reason to get a card with an annual fee. There are plenty of cards on the market that do not charge an annual fee.

However, once you become a credit card expert you may find a card that works well for you and charges a fee. I will only consider a credit card with an annual fee if I can get that annual fee back in some sort of reward meaningful to us. I consider a credit card fee an investment in that card, and I expect a return on that investment. For example, we currently hold two credit cards and one of them has a fee of $99 and the other is free. We use the $99 card for most purchases so we can rack up travel miles for future travel. Because we use it for all our purchases, we receive a voucher each year that more than compensates us for the $99 fee through travel benefits or companion fares. Do the math to ensure you get a return on your annual fee, otherwise it is not worth it. As a side note, we have *never* paid more than $99 for a card. You may find cards that charge hundreds of dollars, and I find little financial reason for it.

Cash Advances

Credit card companies make many things easy for you, including using ATMs for cash advances against your credit card. In fact, they allow you to gain access to cash by using your credit card and a PIN, just like a debit card. But the credit card is far from a debit card.

When you sign up for a credit card, you'll receive a cardholder agreement that provides details about the card, including fees and other charges. Read your cardholder agreement carefully. Typically, card companies will charge you a higher interest rate for cash advances than a standard purchase *and* interest will start on the day you take the advance. At least with standard charges on your credit card, you get a grace period where no interest is charged until your payment is due each month. Not so with cash advances.

Unless you are in a dire situation, do not use your credit card for cash advances. Only your bank debit card should be used for cash.

Foreign Exchange Fees

If you plan on traveling outside of the United States, using your credit card for purchases while traveling can be an excellent way to manage your money. Because the value of our currency is always different than another country's, you should be aware of the exchange rate before you travel. For example, if you are traveling to a country with the Euro as their currency, it may cost $1.25 in our currency to get one Euro. If you are traveling to Australia, you may be able to get $1.30 in Australian dollars for every $1 in American money.

The rates fluctuate daily and can cost you more than just the exchange rate if you don't pay attention to other fees. Credit cards provide you the best foreign currency exchange rate on your purchases, and they allow you to keep smaller amounts of foreign paper currency in your pocket. However, be aware of cards that charge foreign exchange fees, which is a fee for every transaction made in a foreign country. Many times, these fees will be a

> **Knowledge Drop**
>
> The smallest country in the world is Vatican City which is surrounded by Rome, Italy. The country is 0.19 square miles. Conversely, the largest country is Russia measuring in at 6.5 million square miles. In comparison, the United States is 3.8 million square miles

percentage of your transaction and add up very quickly.

Debit cards will generally have foreign transaction fees and are less useful for foreign travel, until you need cash. Review the cardholder agreement to see if a card has any foreign exchange fees. If they don't, credit cards will provide you better and more accurate foreign currency exchange rates than your bank.

If you get cash from your local bank before you leave, they will charge you a fee along with the exchange rate from U.S. dollars into the currency you need. If you use your debit card at a foreign ATM, you will be charged those same fees by your bank, plus fees from the bank that owns the ATM.

Even on a short trip to another country, these fees can add up quickly, so plan ahead. Typically, we will research our destination to see how frequently credit cards are used in the area. We will take small amounts of cash in case we run across vendors, stores, or transportation options that do not accept credit cards. Review how much your local bank will charge you to get foreign currency before you leave. Many times, it is cheaper to find a foreign ATM upon arrival to get the small amount of cash you need.

The same credit card rules apply for travel. Make sure you are following your budget and tracking all your expenses, so that you can pay off your bill when you get back home. Just because you're globetrotting doesn't mean you throw away all your spending rules. Using your credit card as a loan to fund your vacation is not a good financial plan.

Reconciling your Statement

As we discussed in the budgeting chapter, each time you make a purchase, you should enter it into your money software program. Each purchase should be dropped into the appropriate money bucket, so you know what you spend from each bucket over time.

Each month, you should review your credit card statement to match it with your transactions in the money software program. This will ensure you captured all the transactions for the month, but also be sure there were no fraudulent transactions made on your card.

Credit Card Fraud

Unfortunately, credit card fraud and identity theft are becoming more prevalent in our world. Your card information can be stolen many ways, including hacking into a vendor that has your card information or through skimming machines on terminals where you use your cards. The good news is many credit card companies have become experts at recognizing fraudulent transactions and are quick to take action. If you have done nothing negligent, the credit card companies will not hold you responsible for card transactions not made by you. To protect yourself, you should follow a few simple rules:

- If your card is ever lost or stolen, you should immediately contact your credit card company. If you don't notify them quickly, the credit card company may hold you accountable for all the charges made.
- Set account alerts on your credit card. You can receive text or email notifications whenever your card is used, if it is used over a certain transaction amount, or if more than one transaction posted to your account.
- When traveling, notify the credit card company through their app or website to let them know where and when you are traveling. This way, when they see a credit card charge in Ames, Iowa when you live in Tempe, Arizona, they will not think it is fraud and shut off your card while on your trip. If they see a charge in London, England when you did not identify any travel, they are more likely to question this charge.
- Track your receipts and reconcile your statement every single month to find any discrepancies.

I have had my credit card number stolen three times. The first time, I have no idea how the number was stolen, but the credit card company caught it and called me right away. They asked me to verify a charge, which I did not make. They immediately canceled the card and sent me a new one.

The second time, I was playing basketball at my local gymnasium just like I had for the previous ten years. I changed my clothes in the locker room and left my work clothes (along with my wallet and keys) in a locker with a combination lock. No one other than me knew the combination. After completing my workout, I walked into the locker room and one of my friends told me to check my things because they had some items stolen. I told him mine were locked with a combination lock. He said his was, too. At that time, my wallet held one credit card and one bank card. The bank card was missing. I panicked and immediately called my local bank and had them cancel the card.

> **Knowledge Drop**
>
> According to Intuit, credit card fraud made up a total of 459,297 reported instances of fraud and identity theft combined in 2020. Instances of identity theft by credit card fraud increased by an alarming 44.6% from 2019 to 2020.

About thirty minutes later, I received a call from my credit card company, asking me if I had just made a $600 charge at a Vonn's grocery store in California. My heart sank and I felt like I was going to throw up. Obviously, I had not made the charge and after explaining the whole incident to the credit card company, they removed the charges from my account and canceled the card. Whoever stole my credit card number was a professional. They knew how to pick my combination lock and gain access to my wallet. Then, they stole my bank card as a diversion, knowing full well that I would cancel the card that was missing, not the one that was still in my wallet. All the while, they took the credit card number off the card that was still in my wallet and tried to use it. After that day, I never brought my wallet to the gym ever again.

The third time, I was finishing up an event with some customers of mine in Scottsdale, Arizona. I had just handed my credit card to the waiter to take care of the bill. As he disappeared back into the kitchen, I received a phone call from a representative at my credit card company asking me if I had just used my card. With surprise, I said I literally just handed it to the waiter. Then they asked if I was in Las Vegas. Obviously, I was not. Someone had just used my card number at a restaurant, but the credit card flagged it as fraudulent activity. I thanked them for being so quick and professional while they canceled my current card and promised to send me a new one right away. As I hung up the phone, I quickly realized I had just handed my card to the waiter, and he was about to run a card that had just been canceled. The timing was impeccable.

Looking back on that third time, I believe my card number was stolen from a skimming machine installed at a credit card terminal on a gas pump. Crooks have small devices they can plug into the swiping portion of a terminal that will automatically read your number as it is being charged by the vendor. Never use a credit card terminal that looks like it has been tampered with or if it is difficult to slide your card in. The terminal may have a skimming machine. You can also Google "what does a skimming device look like?" and it will show you, so you can be on the lookout.

Debit vs. Credit

When you have a checking account with a financial institution, more than likely your account comes with a bank card. This bank card can be used for debit transactions or credit transactions, and it is important to recognize the difference. A debit transaction requires you to enter a PIN to complete the transaction. A debit transaction does not have the same fraud protection as credit card transactions I described earlier, so when using your bank card for purchases, always choose the option for a credit transaction. Many times, the transaction will automatically ask you for a PIN but there is always an override to make the transaction a credit.

When using a bank card, whether it is a debit or credit transaction, the impact on your bank account is the same. The money will come out right away. The difference is fraud protection for you. If you use your bank card for a debit transaction and your number is hacked, you may be responsible for those fraudulent charges. With credit transactions, the company will be responsible.

I know this can be confusing, but this issue only applies to bank cards. Credit cards only allow credit transactions, and you will receive fraud protection.

Becoming a Credit Card Expert

Once you are well on your way up the Financial Pyramid by following the guidelines in this book, including staying within your budget, tracking all your expenses, fully funding your uh-oh fund, saving for retirement, and paying off your credit card bill every single month, then you may consider using your credit cards a different way. However, the only way this works is when you have your financial house in order.

My wife and I have three financial cards in our wallets: two credit cards and a bank card. Our concept is we want every single transaction we make to provide us a reward in return. Every possible transaction should have a purpose in helping us to accomplish our goal or reward. When we make purchases, we get points or credit for something in return. There is an endless supply of reward cards out there that provide you things such as airline miles, hotel points, discounted merchandise, cash back, and cash back deferred to a 529 plan. The key is to determine which goal is most important to you, find a card that helps you achieve your goal, and then put every single possible charge on that card.

Again, this only works if you have your financial house in order and you follow these rules:

- You pay off your credit card balance every single month. Have I said you should pay off your card every single month?

- Stay within your budget. This credit card strategy does not allow you to spend money willy-nilly just so you can rack up points for a free flight to Tahiti or cash back for a new TV. This strategy allows you to get something in return for your "normal day-to-day charges."
- Do not pay an annual fee on a rewards credit card unless you get a return on that investment. If you cannot, then the card is not worth it. We have never paid more than $99 for a card, but we get it back in a free or deeply discounted flight on top of the regular points we receive for other travel. I have seen annual fees on travel cards that exceed $500 – which is just ludicrous.
- Do not charge anything to your credit card that costs you extra money to use your credit card. For example, some utilities or property taxes will allow you to use your credit card for payment but will add a surcharge to your payment to do so. They are trying to charge you back the credit card fees they are charged by the credit card company for using your card. Don't fall for it! Our cell phone provider gives us a monthly discount of $5 per line if we use our bank card instead of our credit card. We will forego credit card points for a discounted rate.

In our house, travel is important to us, so we chose a primary credit card that helps us rack up airline miles that we can use for airline tickets, vacation packages, or hotel stays. We chose the American Airlines card because we live in a hub city for American and we fly with them most of the time. Typically, with an airline card you will get bonus miles if you use their card to buy airline tickets on their airline. With American, we receive one mile for every dollar we spend, but if we buy something from American, we get two miles for every dollar.

Our second credit card is with Costco. Why? To understand, let's discuss Costco's business strategy. Costco wants to have low pricing, which means they need a very low-cost structure. They achieve this throughout their organization by selling products inside a big, no-frills warehouse, staging products straight from a forklift, and selling in large, lower cost quantities. Have you ever tried to find an employee to help you find where they moved the peanut butter? Nope. During the day, all their employees are where they have the highest impact – taking your money. All of it is focused on high efficiency and low cost, which is great for us because we buy things at a low cost and great for them because they earn a profit from it.

This style can also be seen with how they take payments. Remember earlier when we discussed how credit card companies make money by charging merchants whenever credit cards are used at their store? Well Costco wants to control those fees, so many stores only take debit cards. The fee to use them is substantially lower. The only exception is when you use the Costco card (managed by Citi), because a portion of those credit card fees are being filtered back to Costco so they can make more money. In return, you get to buy products that are only marked up by say fifteen percent or less. At other retail grocery stores, these markups could be as high as fifty percent or more.

Well, we spend enough money at Costco that I want to make those purchases count for something else and paying with my debit card gets me nothing. We got the no annual fee Costco card that we use for all our Costco purchases, and we receive a percentage of cash back for those purchases. Every year we receive a check from Costco for the purchases we made in the previous year, and we use it to buy more things at Costco. This allows Costco to gain in two more ways. Let's pretend that we got $100 cash back from using their card. We just go buy a $100 worth of goods and give that money right back to Costco. And we bought $100 worth of products that only cost them roughly $85 (because they markup their products by approximately fifteen percent). And we racked up this cash back by using their card where a percentage of the purchase goes back to Costco. Wow – Costco really has their stuff together.

Additionally, we can use the Costco card as a backup if our American card gets lost, stolen, or just is not working for some reason.

Our plan is to put every available purchase on the American card, all Costco purchases are put on the Costco card, and everything else is paid through our checking account by way of check, bank card, Zelle, Venmo, or other cash transferring service. Every possible charge gets something in return. One time when we bought a car, we wanted to make a large cash down payment. We put the down payment on the credit card to get miles, and then used the cash to pay off the credit card charge.

No matter how hard you try, there are certain things you cannot put on a credit card. Some are restricted and others just do not make sense to charge, such as:

- Loan or mortgage payments are restricted because loan companies want to be sure you have the cash and are not just racking up more debt.
- Income taxes are restricted.
- Homeowners Associations can be paid by credit card but will typically charge a fee to do so.
- Property taxes may be paid by credit card but will typically charge a fee to do so.
- Cash gifts for birthdays, weddings, or funerals. However, we have started buying gift cards instead of providing cash. Then, we can use our credit card to pay for the gift.
- Some vendors may require you to use a bank draft to pay, such as our electric company. Other vendors may offer a sizable discount to not use a credit card, such as our cell phone company.
- Some contractors may offer you a “cash price” and “credit price” so they can save on the merchant credit card fees. In fact, we ask many contractors if they have a cash price to save a little money.
- If you are betting on horses during the Kentucky Derby at Churchill Downs, you will need cash because they do not take credit cards. So I’ve heard.

Chapter 28

Controlling Your Benjamins, Because Benjamin Would Want It That Way

Benjamin Franklin famously said, "A penny saved is a penny earned." Saving a penny can also include not spending it irrationally. There have been times where someone in my family will come home from the store with an unplanned purchase in hand. They immediately rationalize that they saved us money because it was "on sale." No matter how much you rationalize, it is impossible to spend money and save money at the exact same time. You either spent money or you did not.

Every dollar you earn should be saved, spent, or donated in the best way possible. When you have a dollar in your hand or in your bank account, think about the most productive way to use that dollar – save, spend, or donate.

How to productively spend the dollar is typically the area most people have a problem with. Spending is a balancing act between handling the things you need (food, shelter, clothing), and the things you desire (junk food, a new phone, a luxury car). Some get into financial trouble because they do not distinguish between the needs and wants and spend without reason or discipline. Every time you spend money on a want that was not productive, you lost the opportunity to use it for something better.

Throughout your life, every hard-earned dollar you spend should be done with scrutiny. This is especially critical when you are younger, and your financial resources are more limited. If you live day to day by spending uncontrollably and without a financial plan, it will be very tough to move up the Financial Pyramid. Buy things you need and buy things you want (within your budget), but buy them with discipline.

Why do things cost what they cost?

The pricing of the products and services we buy depends on numerous factors. For a business, the ultimate price of a product or service is the price that someone is willing to pay and nothing less.

I participated in a business meeting once where a presenter talked about how to price goods and services. He demonstrated his views by talking about buying a Miller Lite in Las Vegas.

> **Knowledge Drop**
>
> Ben Franklin was quick witted with many funny quotes, but a favorite of mine is "If you would not be forgotten as soon as you are dead and rotten, either write things worth reading, or do things worth writing." – *Poor Richard's Almanac.*

Imagine you are standing in a casino and wanting a Miller Lite. The casino has no problem providing you a Miller Lite. In fact, they are hoping you will have several so you damage your decision-making skills and lose your hard-earned funds while gambling. Anyway, while standing in the casino you could walk fifty to a hundred yards in any direction and you could easily find a beer. But do you think they are all priced the same? No way. The casino is betting on the fact (pun intended), that you are not going to walk around completing your due diligence to find the lowest priced can or bottle of Miller Lite.

Here is an example of how different locations within the same casino could price the exact same beer:

- Bar without a food menu = $5.00
- Bar with food menu = $6.50
- Sit down restaurant = $7.50
- Mini bar in your room = $8.50
- While gambling at the slots = FREE

A casino will take advantage of the situation to maximize their profits at your expense. My point is that a little due diligence on the goods and services you buy can save you money – sometimes a little, sometimes a lot. Over a lifetime, dollars add up if you buy things you don't need or overpay on the things you do. A few guidelines to follow:

- Identify if the purchase is a want or a need.
- Evaluate your wants and determine if your purchase is worth the money. Why do you want this product or service? Is it an impulse buy? Is it within your budget? Are there similar or the same products at a better price?
- Compare pricing and quality of the products and services you buy.
- More expensive does not guarantee better quality.
- Get at least three quotes on big purchases.
- Do not assume the last place you bought something is still cheaper – even Amazon or Costco.

Living on the leading edge of technology

Technology is awesome, because in most cases it makes our lives easier and better. Just thinking about how technology has changed our lives in a short period of time is mind boggling. We can ride in a self-driving car, send money instantly to our friends with a touch of an app, talk to friends through a watch, and tell a speaker in our home to order toilet paper. We went from going to a video store for a VHS tape, to getting DVDs delivered in the mail, to streaming anything we want from home with the push of a button.

Technology is awesome and fun but has also become essential in our day-to-day activities. Consider our time during the pandemic where we needed access to Wi-Fi and computers so our kids could go to school, or we could go to work virtually, or we could connect through a video call with our family and friends. Primary communications and registration for vaccine appointments were sent through social media, which left people without technology at a significant disadvantage.

Technology surrounds us whether we like it or not and changes our world quickly. New technology is thrown at us daily and we must decide if it's a technology we *need* vs. *want*. Living on the leading edge of every technological advancement can be expensive and a waste of money.

Knowledge Drop

According to a study by McAfee, 43% of people went on vacation with the intent to unplug from technology. Of those, 81% reported having a more enjoyable vacation because of the lack of connectivity.

A few years ago, I had an employee try to talk me into installing an instant messaging app on all our computers so employees could immediately correspond with each other. I was a bit frustrated with the request, responding, "Right now, people can reach you by email, text, calling the phone sitting on your desk, calling the phone in your pocket, or simply walking into your office. How many more ways do we need to distract you from your work?" The app got his interest because it was new and shiny. I get it. Some technology is great, but we need to evaluate if the technology we are buying (and buying *into*) is worth it. Are we buying the technology to improve our lives in some way, or are we buying technology because it's the next shiny object that catches our attention? Here are some examples of questions to ponder while evaluating whether to buy the latest and greatest technology:

- Why buy a brand-new television with the latest technology when there are very few programs broadcast in that new technology? Why not wait a year or more when the programming has caught up and the technology is much cheaper?

- Why buy a $600 smart watch when the phone in your pocket can pretty much do all the same things?
- How many features on your smart phone do you actually use? How many features do you need? Is it worth it to buy the next generation of a phone immediately upon its launch? Buying last year's version or waiting sometime after the launch of a new product can save you a bunch of money and you really don't lose any functionality.
- Why buy the fastest and most expensive internet on the market when a lower speed will work just as well, or your equipment can only handle a fraction of the speed? How much do you need to run your current devices?
- Do you need all the features of your current cell phone plan, or can you get away with a lower cost option? We were paying extra for a mobile hotspot feature we hardly ever used. Also evaluate the amount of data you use. It is nice to have an unlimited plan, but are there lower cost options still within your usage?
- There are plenty of options to add technology in your home such as a camera at your front door or in your refrigerator, the ability to operate your garage door or thermostat from a remote location, or talking to an inanimate object to order you things on the internet. Some of this technology is great for safety and other things are just convenient. How much are you paying for the convenience? Is there an upfront charge along with a monthly subscription? Is the convenience worth it, or could that money be spent in a more productive place, like savings?

Living on the leading edge of technology can be fun and exciting. Just know it can also be costly. If the technology is important to you, then have at it. Just scrutinize your purchases to ensure you are doing it for the right reasons. Also know that once you start using a convenience, it is hard to go back to a world without it. Only embrace new technology that makes your life easier and more productive.

How to evaluate quotes

Whenever my wife and I need to make a sizable purchase, we do some comparison shopping. The comparison is not just about price, it can also be about the features of the product or service we are buying. The purchases can range in size from a home remodel to buying a new office chair, and everything in between. First, we make a list of things that are important to us about the product. For example, if we are buying a new phone, we may want a certain size of storage to even consider a product. Then, we make a list of other things critical to a purchase that may include the warranty, delivery time frame, and customer reviews. As we research different businesses, we make notes next to our list so we can compare each company equally.

For an example, let's say that we need to get our house painted. We really are not pressed for time to get the painting done, but when they start work, we want it done quickly. It's also very important that a high-quality paint is used and can stand up to the brutal summers we have in Arizona. Our comparison list could look something like this:

	Painter#1	Painter#2	Painter#3
Type of paint			
Quality of paint			
Warranty of paint			
Warranty of work			
References			
Years in business			
Time frame to start			
Time to finish			
Price			

This process can be used for any product or service you buy. Make a list of things that are "must haves" for the product or service and a list of things that are important but not deal breakers. Then, get quotes from contractors or businesses and detail the specifics for your list.

One of the critical points in comparison shopping is ensuring the things you're comparing are identical or very similar. If you find two products or services with dramatically different prices, then you should validate the price. Do not automatically just pick the lowest price! For example, it is pointless to compare pricing between two cell phones where one has 64 gig of memory and the other has 256 gig of memory. A true comparison will show phones with the same memory and similar features.

I would say much of the time, we buy products or services toward the middle of the road in price. We may not choose the lowest price because we do not want to forego certain features, and we may not choose the highest price because we feel comfortable that we can get everything we need for a lower cost. Many companies try to sell their products or services at a higher cost due to "value" or name recognition that comes with large marketing budgets. You just need to determine whether the increased cost is worth the value as presented.

Other random ways to effectively reduce expenses

- **Eat in instead of eating out.** I hate this one, but it is true. Money can leak out of your budget quickly for those daily coffees, morning bagels, happy hours, or family dinners at a restaurant. Monitor your expenses in this area and set a goal of reducing it by just a little bit each month. Twenty bucks is still twenty bucks!
- **Gym memberships.** Your health is important, so if you use your gym membership regularly, then keep it. To be clear, regularly means two or more times per week, not once per year. I have read a lot on the topic and paying for a gym membership alone does not make you healthier – you have to use the equipment at the gym. Also consider what you do

at the gym that you cannot do at home or in the park. If you run to stay in shape and live in a cold climate, maybe only utilize the gym membership during the winter months so you can run on the treadmill frostbite free.

- **Happy hour shenanigans.** Just so you know, when you go out with a large group of people and everyone is on the same bill, somebody is going to get screwed. Inevitably, one of the following things happen:
  - The person that had the most drinks oversees divvying out the bill. This is not a good time to do math.
  - One person who does not track money or think it is worth the time says, "Let's just split it evenly." Everyone else quickly falls in line because they do not want to be seen as "that guy" or the cheapskate. Sometimes splitting the bill is fine unless you specifically did not eat an appetizer and stuck to the cheap beer instead of an expensive cocktail to save money.

This is a no-win situation. If you are on a tight budget, or just tight (like me), there are a couple strategies I have used to get around this.

If the group sat down together, then state up front to the server that you would like a separate check and point who is in your party. This works, but it isn't the preferred method because it can be hard on the wait staff and they may spit in your food.

A second strategy is if you arrive earlier or later than the rest of the group, go directly to the bar to order and pay for your food and drink. This will cause you to get up and walk to the bar when it comes time to order more, but you did cancel that gym membership so the exercise will do you good. You're welcome. I just increased your steps for today.

- **Cut the cord.** Move away from the expensive television broadcasting services where you plug a cable into the wall. There are a ton of alternatives based on your entertainment wants. However, if you sign up for every lower cost streaming subscription available, you'll end up paying more than cable. Do the math and pay attention to those ongoing price increases that may outprice the value of whatever broadcasting service you are using.

- **Get local channels for free (kind of).** If you really want to go on the cheap, buy a TV antenna for less than $15 and get several over the air HD quality TV channels. I was shocked to find that my city has 91 channels available just by adding an antenna. And the quality of the broadcast was surprisingly excellent. However, a few of those are the home shopping network. Please block those channels, especially at 2 o'clock in the morning after happy hour shenanigans.
- **Cell phones.** See the section about living on the leading edge of technology. I highly recommend buying later generation, mid-quality cell phones when a newer model is hitting the shelves. And this is only when you actually need a new phone. You do not need a new phone annually – I know this is crazy talk for many of you, but it's true. Shop around for deals on phones because your cell phone carrier may not be the best place to buy a new phone.
- **Data plans.** Shop carriers and features of a data plan that works for you. For example, we switched our unlimited plan to a cheaper plan and basically only lost the ability to use our phones as mobile hot spots. We seldom used that feature, so it wasn't worth the extra money to us.
- **Wi-Fi plans.** The key here is to make sure you only pay for what you need. Many businesses try selling laser fast plans that you may not need. Do some research before paying for the highest tier because it makes you feel better. Also, even though you may pay for the highest tier, that doesn't guarantee you will actually get the speed offered. Do some research.
- **Go to the store with a list.** I see you impulse buyers who go to the grocery store hungry and come out with five bags of chips and three candy bars. Make a list and stick to it. This is not just for the grocery store – it's for *any* store. If you need a new pair of shorts because the recent pandemic caused

> **Knowledge Drop**
>
> According to a survey by Field Agent, 56% of respondents said they always, or usually use a list when shop for groceries. 17% said they rarely or never do.

your current ones to shrink, then go to the store for shorts. Do not walk out with a pair of sandals and a shirt to go with it. This is especially dangerous for places like Costco. I am specifically speaking to a close family member of mine that has been married for over 25 years to a wonderful, caring person, who also happens to now be an author.

- **Check insurance quotes annually.** Review and compare insurance policies for your auto and home each year. They can sometimes fluctuate widely when insurance companies want to enter or leave a specific market. Also, it is a good idea to check with an agent to ensure your coverage amounts make sense. Auto and home policies have many different coverage options which can make them complicated, so when evaluating premiums make sure the policy sizes are equal so you can get good pricing comparisons. I typically create a spreadsheet detailing the coverages and pricing for each, so I know the coverages are equivalent.
- **Raise your insurance deductible.** If your financial house is in order and you are higher up on the Financial Pyramid, consider increasing the size of your auto or home deductibles. Increasing a deductible from $1,000 to $2,500 or even $5,000 can lower your insurance premiums considerably, but you need to be prepared to pay the increased deductible if something bad happens. This is only a good idea when your uh-oh fund is fully funded and you have adequate cash on hand. Don't do it just to lower your insurance premiums and then hope for the best. Be prepared to pay your deductible.
- **Bank fees.** There is no reason to pay bank fees unless you made a mistake with an overdraft. If you are paying bank fees, identify why so you can have the account without fees or find a different bank where you can live fee free.

- **Public library.** Find and use your public library for books you want to read via hard copy or electronic version. It is easy and free.
- **Secondhand stores.** Secondhand stores are not only a great place for donations, but are also excellent places to find clothes, furniture, and dishes at low prices. It's also a sustainable way to benefit the environment by recycling. There are some consignment stores where you can find excellent pricing, also.

Donations

If you have your financial house in order, specifically if you are paying all your bills on time and established an uh-oh fund, then look at where you can budget and donate money to those in need. If you do not have your financial backroom in order, you can always find places to donate time or other resources such as a special expertise you can offer. Many non-profits need help with things like manual labor, marketing, or fundraising that only cost you time.

Helping others is an important part of life. Not only is it kind and generous but is also helps your mental health. It feels good to help others. When you can offer a financial gift, find someplace that strikes passion for you and offer up something, even if it is small. Just make sure you know the organization and that the money is going where you think it is.

Unfortunately, there are too many scams out there where people will give a tear-jerking story through a Go Fund Me page or some other fund-raising mechanism to raise funds and it turns out to not be true. Instead, your cash is just padding the pockets of the page owner.

One Saturday morning, I was watching ESPN's College Game Day which was taking place at my alma mater, before a big football game. There was a guy who stood behind the College Game Day stage on live television with a sign jokingly asking for more Busch Light. He included his Venmo account information. And people donated. And donated. And donated. I find this a bit sad that people will just send their money to this guy for a joke. But the story takes a positive turn. This guy received so much money it became embarrassing for him, so he donated the money to a children's hospital. When that story hit, people donated even more to him. He ended up donating over a million dollars to the hospital – all over a sign asking for beer. When humans put their mind to something, we can really make things happen.

> **Knowledge Drop**
>
> For whatever reason, the state of Iowa has claimed Busch Light as their favorite beer. I am very proud of the state where I grew up, but I whole heartedly disagree with their beer choice.

Even though the story turned out well, please do not donate your hard-earned money to some random guy you see on the TV asking for beer.

If we are donating to an organization, I will try to do research and see how much of the organization's budget is used for administrative costs versus the actual cause. Even though people deserve to make a good wage while running non-profits, I do not want to fund exorbitant salaries or overhead costs. I want to make a difference in the cause.

To ensure our money is used for a good purpose, we have sometimes earmarked funds for a specific purpose instead of just donating to a general fund where you really do not know where the money goes. Examples of this could include buying books for the elementary school library, updating technology at your church, or buying specific band instruments for the high school marching band. We always feel a bit better if we are donating for a thing or a person, instead of just dropping money into an organization's general account. If you are interested in this type of philosophy, then ask the organization what they specifically need. I have found they have no problem sharing a detailed list with you so you can pick a specific cause.

Another way to donate money is through a random act of kindness. We usually do this as a family between Thanksgiving and Christmas. Each family member will get a sum of money that can be given to whomever they want, but it must be done anonymously. This could be for a friend in need, a family member, or our favorite barista. I remember one Christmas, one of our daughters wanted to give her $50 bill to an extremely nice waitress we always saw at a frequented restaurant. My daughter wrote a card to the waitress saying how nice she was and that we wanted to thank her with this gift. She placed the money inside the card, and we asked the restaurant's manager if she would give the card to the waitress, but not tell her where it came from. About twenty minutes later, the manager came back to our table with a huge smile on her face. She told us that the waitress was so happy she started to cry. The waitress was going to school to become a nurse and the money would be very helpful to her.

Recently we a bought a gift card at our frequented coffee shop and gave it back to the barista. We asked him to use the money to pay it forward. A couple of days later, he told us that it was amazing providing free drinks to the patrons and many of them added money to the gift card themselves. He was visibly excited to participate in the process.

During the COVID-19 pandemic I signed up for a volunteer shift at a vaccine distribution site. I really wanted to find a way to help others during this difficult time, but by volunteering it also gave me the opportunity to get vaccinated, which was important to me. I was amazed at how participating in the volunteer opportunity made me feel. I felt like I was contributing to society in an important way, and the people getting vaccinated were so happy and relieved they were getting their shots. It was so impactful to me that I volunteered again.

There are many ways to show kindness by donating money or time. The key is making just a bit of effort to make the most of your gift that is precious to others. There will be something in it for you, too.

Chapter 29

Buying a New Ride Without Getting Taken for a Ride

Buying a car is generally one of the first big purchases of someone's life. Cars are important in our lives because we need them to get to and from work or school, run errands, taxi your children around, and drive to your vacation destination. Buying a car can be exciting and fun in between all the monotony of the research and the anxiety of negotiations. This chapter will provide some guidelines on buying a car and identify traps that can cost you hundreds, if not thousands, of dollars.

Fresh out of college and with a job offer in hand, my dad and I set out to buy a new car for my new life as a tax paying adult. My Toyota Celica that got me through college had well over 100,000 miles and I was not sure it would get me where I needed to go over the next year. My new job required me to move from Iowa to Arkansas for a few months before I would be permanently assigned somewhere else in the United States. I needed a good dependable ride for the upcoming moves. Besides getting a job that started my career, buying a new car was the next steppingstone to adulting and putting on my big boy pants.

I settled on a gray 1992 Chevy Lumina, two door coupe from a large car dealership near Des Moines. I loved that car. Probably because it was the first real adulting financial move of my life and it was mine. My dad did cosign on the loan, but I paid every penny for that car on my own. You see, I was twenty-two and fresh out of college with a job offer, but I had not received my first paycheck yet. I had no real credit to speak of and no assets. So, understandably, the bank was a bit leery of loaning me money outright, so they asked my dad to cosign the loan. This means if I missed payments or defaulted on the loan, they could go after him to pay for it. I never missed a payment. Looking back, that car was probably the equivalent of the family truckster from National Lampoon's Vacation, but I still miss driving it.

Researching vehicles back then was pretty much done on the car lot with a sales guy paid by commission following you around. I do not remember much negotiating, but I do remember getting discounts for being a first-time car buyer and being a college graduate. I could never know for sure if we got a great deal, but the salesperson was quite exasperated by the end of the transaction, and I could tell he was done with us. I think what put him over the edge is when I asked if he could replace the donut spare tire with a real one. He was not having any of it. His face turned red, and he shook his head slowly side to side saying, "There is no money left in this deal." I think I saw a tear in his eye.

A Car is an Asset, Just Not a Good One

The best assets are ones where you get a return on your investment. A car is an asset where that will never happen. However, unless you live in a large city with public transportation opportunities, or if you work from home, a car is a needed form of transportation.

Unfortunately, if you purchase a brand-new car, the minute you drive it off the car lot, it is immediately worth less than what you just paid. Cars go down in value quickly, so it's important that you pay particular attention to which car you buy, how much you pay, how you pay for it, and how you maintain it.

Because poor buying decisions can cost you large amounts of money over the time you own a vehicle, put work in up front by saving for a down payment, identifying your budget, establishing your car needs, researching cars meeting those requirements, and knowing possible financing options.

How Much Can You Afford?

Back in the year 2000, the state of Arizona went through a painful process forever dubbed the "Alt Fuels Fiasco." The reality is, it had less to do with alternative fuels and more to do with a law put in place by our omnipotent law makers. Basically, to promote alternative fuels, they developed a program that would compensate vehicle owners to convert gasoline burning engines to alternative fuels. The goal was to reduce our dependence on foreign-bought oil and improve emissions quality of the vehicles in Arizona. Sounds like a great program, right? People can affordably get behind alternative fuels, we help the environment, and reduce our dependence on foreign oil. That is a win, win, win. Well, the devil is in the details.

The law said car owners would be compensated by the state government for fifty percent of the new vehicle cost and for the cost of the conversion from gas to the alternative fuel. How awesome is that? Consumers got half of the car paid for by the government (through our taxes) and then the government also paid for the conversion (through our taxes). And get this: the tank holding the alternative fuel only had to be one gallon in size *and* there was no requirement you had to run the vehicle on the alternative fuel. Wait, what? It's okay to go back and read that sentence again. Yep – the state created a law where they would subsidize fifty percent of a new vehicle cost and a conversion, but not actually require you to use it. Your tax dollars at work, ladies and gentlemen. But it gets better.

The state estimated this subsidy would cost a few million dollars. Well, the citizens of Arizona quickly saw the "free" dollars that paid for half of a new car purchase, and they jumped on the band wagon.

Car dealerships were ecstatic, alternative fuels conversion shops were rolling in the dough, and anyone "needing" a new car was euphoric. The program ended up costing the state close to one billion dollars. That is right, one billion with a "B."

I see you're getting flustered – what does this story have to do with buying a car? Patience, Grasshopper. Well, after the state's check printer ran out of ink for the hundredth time because it wrote $1 billion worth of checks, the state pulled the plug on the program. After the program was canceled, one of the local news stations did an interview with a married couple that made me so angry, I still remember it over twenty years later. The couple had just bought a brand-new top-of-the-line Ford Expedition (an expensive vehicle) with the intent of participating in the alternative fuels program, which meant the government would subsidize half of the cost of the vehicle. But since the government just announced this gravy train was over, the couple was complaining that by ending this program, they would now have to pay for the whole car (gasp) all by themselves! In turn, this was going to put them in dire straits because they could no longer afford the vehicle. Personal responsibility, people! Yes, I realize that the law was the law and people should be able to take advantage of it. But when it became crystal clear it was a stupid law, and that people were taking advantage of the program only for their personal gain (getting a new car instead of helping the environment), you had to know something had to give. And these people bought a car they couldn't afford in the first place.

> **Knowledge Drop**
>
> Government subsidies paid to you are not "free" money. You paid the government money by way of taxes, and they are filtering it back.

By developing and maintaining your budget, as well as following other guidelines in this book, you should be able to determine how much you can reasonably afford. Make sure your uh-oh fund is in place and you have saved up some amount of money for a down payment on a car loan before moving forward.

The best way to save money on a vehicle is to buy used instead of new and buy it with cash. The value of a car decreases the greatest amount right after it is purchased new. By purchasing a vehicle a few years old, you can take advantage of a much more reasonable price while the car is still in good working order. Additionally, the drop in value will not be as significant immediately after purchase.

If you can buy the vehicle with cash, then you don't have to be concerned with the costs of a loan and making those pesky payments. However, I will not ignore the fact that car loans are generally essential in purchasing a vehicle particularly earlier in life when your earning potential and savings are at a lower level.

> **Knowledge Drop**
>
> According to numerous industry experts, the value of a new car declines by about 10% the moment you drive it off the lot. The first year will see a 20% decline followed by 10%-15% every year after.

There is an endless supply of ways to research used vehicles for their quality and pricing, along with numerous ways to find vehicles from private sellers near you. Buying a used vehicle at a car dealership may be easier but will also come at a higher price. They must pay for that nice showroom somehow! Buying a vehicle from a private party can save you some money, but it also is more time consuming and can be a bit of a hassle.

A Car's Cost is More Than Just a Payment

A common mistake in car buying is to only focus on the car payment. I understand that a car payment is the pain point and the biggest concern impacting your immediate finances. However, by ignoring other facets of buying a car you can unknowingly be wasting money or be surprised by costs at some point down the road. In the next section we will discuss how to structure a car loan. Beyond that, here are some other financial impacts to consider when researching which car to buy:

- **Sales tax:** On top of the sales price of your new vehicle, there will be the appropriate sales tax for the city and state in which you buy the vehicle.
- **Car insurance:** Insurance for you and your car is a must, not only because it is required by law, but because it is a smart thing to do. Car insurance will provide financial security in case of an accident caused by you or others. However, it can also put a big dent in your budget. Factors that impact your insurance premiums include:
    - Age of the drivers: Typically, the younger or less experienced drivers will have higher premiums. When we added our teenage driver (a female with good grades who went through a driving school) to our policy, the premiums doubled.
    - Type of car: The car make and model impact your insurance premiums. Cars that have superior safety features and crash ratings will have lower premiums. Cars that are expensive to replace due to their value will have higher premiums. Also, insurance companies review which cars are statistically more likely to be stolen and your premiums will increase accordingly for those cars.
    - Driving record: Drivers with accidents or moving violations will be identified by insurance companies as a higher risk and will have higher premiums.
    - Yearly mileage: The higher number of miles you generally use your vehicle equates to higher opportunities for accidents or moving violations.
    - Credit history: As we discussed earlier in the book, insurance companies will review the credit histories of the insured and will offer lower premiums to those with excellent credit histories.
- **Gas mileage:** Consider how far you'll drive the car and under what conditions. Will you drive on interstates, rural roads, city streets, in stop and go traffic, or long distances? Review the gas mileage for both highway and city driving to understand your gasoline costs. Several years ago, while I

was getting gas, a driver of a large SUV with a below average gas mileage and an above average gas tank pulled up to the pump next to me. I could tell it was a brand-new vehicle because it had a temporary plate on it. I guessed this was the first time the new owner had visited the pump with his vehicle because as it filled with gas, he stood there staring at the gas pump as the dollar signs continued to roll higher and higher. He stared, and stared, and stared. The longer he stared, the more his jaw dropped, and his mouth gaped open. I prepared myself for the fact that I may have to give this guy mouth to mouth when he had his heart attack. It was obvious he was not prepared for the cost of his vehicle.

- **Car registration:** To legally drive your vehicle on public roads, you will need to buy an annual registration from the state you live in. This can be based on the value of your car and can run a few hundred dollars.
- **Maintenance:** Do research to see how dependable the vehicle is and how much common repairs cost. There are online tools that will tell you the average yearly costs or costs over the lifetime of the vehicle. Be warned that several of the most expensive vehicles to buy also come with high maintenance repair price tags. More technology options on a vehicle are awesome, but it also means there are more things that can fail or break.
- **Reliability:** Review how many safety or maintenance recalls may be pending with a particular model or manufacturer. Have there been any failures with the vehicle, either during or after the warranty period? It is very frustrating when you get a new (or used) vehicle where you have numerous ongoing reliability issues, costing you time, money, and peace of mind.
- **Safety:** Understand the safety records and collision testing for the make and models of the vehicles you are considering. Nothing could be worse than buying a vehicle that could put you and your family at risk. Take a break here and Google "Ford Pinto safety."

- **Resale value:** At some point in the future, you are going to want to sell or trade in the vehicle for a different vehicle. Some manufacturers and models hold value better than others and by understanding the resale value, you can save some money when you want to get rid of it. The resale value is generally ignored – at least until you are ready to sell your vehicle. Take this value into account when making your purchasing decision.

The Art of Lowering Your Payments

As the cost of new cars has escalated, car dealerships have become more creative with their marketing gimmicks and finance plans to make car payments more affordable for their customers. Note that I said to make "car payments" more affordable, not the cars themselves. Many finance options can be great opportunities for you to save money but be sure you know the full cost before you make any purchase decisions. Here are a few ways car dealerships have tried to "help" you:

> **Knowledge Drop**
>
> According to Lending Tree, in the year 2021, the average monthly payment for a new car is a whopping $563, while leasing averaged $450, and used cars were an average of $397.

Leasing programs

Car leasing programs have been around forever. In some situations, leasing allows you to obtain a vehicle at a lower monthly payment than if you were to purchase. This is particularly true if you do not have the cash for a down payment. A lease allows you to use a vehicle for a specific time frame, generally 24-, 36-, 48-, or 60-month terms without actually owning it. You operate and maintain the vehicle during the term of the lease and then you can either return the vehicle to the car dealership or buy it outright. In basic terms, the lease payments are determined by the capitalized cost, which is the difference between the sales price and the residual (trade in value) plus interest charges, taxes, and other fees.

For a simplistic example, if the sales price of the car is $25,000 and the trade-in value at the end of the lease is $10,000, the capitalized cost is $15,000 ($25,000 - $10,000). The $15,000 is then financed through the lease, so interest charges and other fees are added on top of the original $15,000, just like any normal loan. That amount will then determine your lease payments.

I do not like leases. In fact, from a financial decision-making standpoint, I can't think of a single reason why leases are a good idea. From an emotional standpoint, there are plenty of reasons to lease a car:

- Lower monthly payments (not necessarily lower overall costs)
- The ability to afford a car you generally could not afford to buy. That is why you see a high number of luxury vehicles under lease.
- The ability to drive a brand-new car every two to five years.

We leased a car once, and we did it poorly. I didn't do enough research about the process and by the time I figured it out, it was too late. It's safe to say I'll never lease another car again. We only focused on the payment instead of negotiating the sales price and trade-in value. We overpaid for the car and the car dealership made quite a bit of money off us. I am okay with businesses making money, just not in a predatory way.

If you ignore the financial logic and move forward with a lease, here is a list of things you should understand if you are contemplating a lease for a car:

- **Complexity:** The car dealerships and finance companies don't want to make the lease terms easy or understandable. From their perspective, the more complex, the better. That way, it is tougher for you to understand the terms and ultimately the cost of the lease.
- **Capitalization Costs:** The capitalization cost is the difference between the sales price of the vehicle and the assumed value of the car at the end of the lease, therefore

determining the amount financed for your lease. Even though this is a lease, you still must negotiate on the sales price of the car. This number *must* be negotiated! Research the sale prices for a comparable make and model car through a third-party website before starting any negotiations with a car dealership. Some dealerships may scam you into making the Manufacturers Recommended Sales Price (MSRP) or sticker price (the price on the sticker in the window of the car) of the vehicle as the sales price, therefore increasing capitalization cost. Don't do it. Negotiate it down to a more reasonable price based on your research.

- **Interest:** Somewhere within the calculation of your lease payments is an interest charge so the car dealership and bank can make more money on the deal. This rate is difficult to find and can easily be hidden in the depths of the lease agreement.
- **Mileage Restrictions:** Lease agreements will detail how many miles per year you can drive the car without penalty. The more miles you drive, the lower the resale value will be at the end of the lease. The car dealerships want to be sure when you return the vehicle it is within an acceptable range so they can resell it for more profit. Be sure to negotiate the mileage you need and understand the penalty for going over the mileage restriction. For example, let's say you have a one-year lease with a mileage restriction of 15,000 miles and a penalty of twenty cents per mile. If after your one-year lease is completed, you return the car with 20,000 miles, you pay a penalty of $1,000 (20,000 actual miles – 15,000 lease miles x $.20 per mile). If you use your vehicle for a high number of miles, a lease is probably not for you.
- **Wear and Tear:** Within the lease, there will be language saying "normal wear and tear" on a vehicle during the lease is acceptable. Anything outside of that will be charged to you when the car is returned. Here is the issue: What is acceptable wear and tear? These terms are vague so there is an opportunity to ding you for additional charges at the end of the lease. Be sure to operate and maintain the vehicle

according to the car's operator's manual and maintenance schedule and keep all the receipts to prove it.

- **Early Termination Fees:** Most leases have a penalty if you return the vehicle sooner than the term of the lease. For instance, if you run into financial problems and want to return the vehicle, there will be additional charges associated with it. Conversely, if you owned a vehicle that was purchased with sound financial decision making, you would be able to sell the vehicle without penalty to receive needed cash.
- **Up Front Costs:** Leases may require you to pay administrative fees or down payments that may or may not impact your monthly payment. Before just writing another check toward the deal, do the math to see how much the lease will cost you over the life of the lease.
- **Other Fees:** Review the lease in detail and ask the car dealership to show you all the other fees associated with the lease. Ultimately, it is your responsibility to know all of these before you sign the lease.
- **Gap Insurance:** When you buy or lease a vehicle with little or no money down, the odds are you will soon owe more money on the vehicle than what it is worth. An issue is created if two weeks after you drive the brand-new car off the lot you get in a bad accident where the car is a total loss. Your insurance company may only pay for the current value of the vehicle instead of what you owe. If your car has a value of $15,000, but you owe $20,000, there is a "gap" or shortage of $5,000 that you will still owe on a car you no longer can drive. Gap insurance will cover that difference. In an ideal world, it is never wise to put yourself in that spot, so hopefully you can make a big enough down payment on the vehicle so that no gap would ever exist. However, if that is not possible, check with your car insurance company for a gap insurance policy. Do *not* buy an insurance policy at the car dealership when it is offered to you. It will be more expensive than if you get one on your own.

Long term financing

Another way car dealerships and finance companies have worked on making payments lower is to extend the term of finance agreements. A typical car loan has a term of 60 months, but in recent years that number has jumped up to 72 or even 84 months. As a comparison, let's assume you are buying a car for $30,000. You made a down payment of $5,000 so you are financing $25,000 at a rate of four percent interest. Below is a comparison of the payments for different loan terms.

Length of Loan (Term)	Monthly Payment
60 months	$460.41
72 months	$391.13
84 months	$341.72

By increasing the term an additional twelve months from 60 to 72 months, your payment would go down by approximately $69 per month. Increase it to 84 months and the payment is almost $120 cheaper than a 60-month loan. But as we have said, it is more than just looking at your payment. Look at the big picture, which means the overall cost of the loan. Here are more details with the same scenarios.

Length of Loan (Term)	Monthly Payment	Total Cost of Loan	Interest Paid
60 months	$460.41	$27,625	$2,625
72 months	$391.13	$28,161	$3,161
84 months	$341.72	$28,704	$3,704

As you can clearly see in the chart above, extending the term and lowering payments costs you quite a bit of money over the term of the loan. A narrow focus of only negotiating a payment may cost you more money in the long run.

Another issue to consider when contemplating a longer-term loan is the resale value of your vehicle. By taking longer to pay off your vehicle, you pay less toward the principal balance of the loan with each payment. This means you'll have less equity in the vehicle (the difference between the value of the vehicle and the amount you owe). In this scenario, it becomes more likely that you will owe more on your vehicle than what it is worth during the term of the loan. If the plan is to keep the vehicle past the term of the loan, this really is not an issue. But if you want to sell or trade in the vehicle before you pay it off, understand that the value may not be higher than what you owe because you have taken so long to pay for the car.

Longer term financing deals can be very enticing at first, but the reality is the impact on your finances can be significant if you do not understand the overall cost of the loan.

What Do You Need in a Ride?

Now that we have determined that this car buying thing is kind of a big deal, let's narrow down which car you are going to buy. The great news is there is no shortage of information at your fingertips to make an informed decision about the car you want to buy. Search "car buying" websites and you will find a long list of options. Be sure to compare three or more of the sites to understand the acceptable price range for the new or used car you want.

First consider all the factors we listed above about MPG, safety, reliability, maintenance, and resale value. Then, go to the next step by identifying which features and options are important such as: two door vs. four door, seating capacity, exterior color, interior color, storage space, cup holders, charging stations – the list goes on and on. You can drown yourself in car options. Make a list of the four or five reasonable options that are most important to you. Since my wife and I live in Arizona and we experience 110-degree heat during the summertime, we steer away from black cars and ensure all the windows are tinted.

Make sure your options list is reasonable. Nicely upgraded rims may look pretty, but are they worth the price? Do you really need a four-wheel drive vehicle? Ask yourself how often you will use it before you commit to the vehicle expense and ongoing maintenance of that option. You are already getting a vehicle with that new car smell, isn't that enough? Also, give your options a priority of importance, just in case the dealership has a car with all your listed options except they don't carry your preferred colors of cardinal and gold to represent your favorite college team. If the color was at the top of your list, then walk away from the deal and find another dealer that respects the Iowa State Cyclones.

After you identify a list of must haves, use your preferred websites to plug in the details to begin comparing different make and models of cars. The best websites will give you a range of pricing and reviews for each car which meet your criteria and budget. Spend some time to narrow the list of possibilities that interest you. Then, find a car dealership nearby that sells the car you are interested in and head on over so you can take a test drive.

> **Knowledge Drop**
>
> According to U.S. News, the new car smell comes from a group of chemicals called volatile organic compounds that can be found in adhesives, fabrics, plastics, and other bits used in the construction of the vehicle.

When you arrive at the car lot, go find the make and model of vehicle you are interested in and begin looking at it. Very quickly, you will be approached by a salesperson wanting to sell you the car. Remember, though: *today is not about buying – today is about researching*. Under no circumstances are you buying a car today. You are only test driving. Make that very clear to the salesperson in a respectful manner.

After you have test driven every car on your narrowed list, it is time to go home, look at your list of cars, and decide. Which car meets your requirements and budget? Research the dealerships in your area to try to find the vehicle you want. Most dealerships will provide a detail of their inventory online where you can research yourself, or you can just send an email to the dealership telling them what you are looking for. Be clear about the vehicle options you absolutely want, along with others that may be optional. Ask the dealership to send you details about the vehicle along with their "out the door" price, meaning the exact amount it will cost you to buy the car. Specifically, you want the overall cost of the car and the financing details available if you purchased the car. This would include the interest rate, term, and payment amount for the loan.

If you live in a metro area, try to get pricing information from at least three dealerships. This may be tougher if you live in a more rural area where obtaining three quotes could cause you to look at dealerships quite a distance from you. In this case, get at least two quotes to make you feel better about the pricing you are getting on your car.

Getting electronic quotes from the dealerships gives you a few advantages. First, you can spend time evaluating and comparing each quote in the comfort of your own home instead of under the gaze of a high-pressure salesperson. Second, by asking for a quote online it will be clear from the dealership that you are looking elsewhere for pricing, so you are more likely to get a favorable deal. Third, this process will be way easier to counteroffer because you are under less pressure than if you were sitting in the dealership. Lastly, you have all the details of the offer in writing, so you have something to fall back on in case a dealership tries to backpedal on their agreed upon terms.

Back in 2010, a large storm tore through a section of Phoenix, causing wind and hail damage in a large swath of the city. Unfortunately, one of our cars was in its path; hail damaged the car beyond repair. Consequently, we were in the market for a new vehicle. I followed the same process I have outlined above. We knew the vehicle we wanted and the price range that vehicle should cost.

I reached out to several dealerships, including one that was about twenty miles from our home. I made it very clear about the process and how they should submit a detailed and complete pricing quote. Soon after, they sent me an email with a quote and details of the car on their lot. After a bit of back and forth, we agreed upon a price that was an acceptable deal and I told them we would come see the car within the hour. If everything was acceptable, we were prepared to buy the car.

> **Knowledge Drop**
>
> According to the National Weather Service Phoenix, the October 2010 hailstorm caused $2.7 billion in insured losses, making it the "costliest storm disaster in the state's history".

We arrived at the dealership, test drove the car, and decided to move forward. Soon after, the dealership provided us a sheet of paper detailing the pricing they were ready to finance. The problem was the pricing on the paper in my hand was different than what they emailed me. After nicely informing them they had made a mistake with the pricing, they backpedaled and gave us some line of bullshit on why the price was different. I told them I was clear over email that they were to provide me their complete pricing and anything different was unacceptable.

They would not uphold their original price, so we immediately stood up and told them we were not buying the car. As we started heading for the door, the salesperson and a manager started chasing us down, asking us to wait and reconsider. I stopped and turned to tell them we would not be buying the car under any circumstances because they had wasted our time and were being deceitful with the pricing. As I turned back toward the front door, two employees stood in front of the door, almost as if they were blocking our exit. This made me even more mad, and I yelled, "Excuse me!" as we passed by. Obviously, with those sales tactics, we would never consider them for another purchase, and I have told that story to anyone looking for that model of car.

After you receive the pricing and options of each available vehicle, plug the details into your preferred car research websites to see how the pricing compares. Because you're viewing cars within a dealership's inventory, you may see varying options from each dealer. This is important to understand when rationalizing the price. If one vehicle has a bigger engine, expect it to have a bigger price tag. That does not necessarily make it a bad deal, as long as you complete your research to make sure it is within an acceptable price range. Most car research websites will give you a range that is a good price for the vehicle to help you understand if you should take the deal, counteroffer, or walk away.

If you want a car from a specific dealership, do not be afraid to counteroffer them to put the car's cost within the acceptable price range. If they are not willing to give a good price, then be prepared to walk away from the deal.

When negotiating over a car, or any other big purchase, always prepare yourself to stop a negotiation if the deal is not right. If you are tied to the transaction with too much emotion, you may be setting yourself up for a bad decision.

The best way to negotiate any deal is to tell yourself it's okay to walk away from the deal – even before the negotiations begin. You would be surprised at how much negotiating power you gain when the other party knows you are willing and able to stop negotiating if certain terms are not met.

Financing Done Right

Know that the easiest place to get a car loan is at the car dealership. Also know that *easy* does not always equate to *better*. While you're researching cars, you should also research financing options. If the car dealership is offering special financing at a low rate, such as 1.9%, then it becomes a no brainer to use their financing. However, if there isn't a low rate, you should shop around for the best interest rate terms. Check with your local bank, credit union, or online banks to get competitive numbers and terms. The interest rate negotiation should be treated like the price of the car. Get competitive quotes for comparison shopping.

What to do With Your Current Car

After researching your new car and the financing, the third requirement is to research your current car, if you are looking to trade it in toward another new or used car. Using the same research tools you used for the new car, evaluate the value of your current car both as a trade-in to the car dealership and as a private sale. Using your current car as a trade-in against a new car is the easiest process, but again, that does not necessarily make it better.

Trading your current car into the dealership allows you to use any equity on the trade-in as a larger down payment, plus you don't have to deal with finding someone to buy your current vehicle. However, more times than not, selling the car yourself will net you a larger amount of money than what a car dealership will offer. A simple website search can give you the value of your car if you were to sell it to a car dealership as a trade-in vs. selling it to a private party. By evaluating the price difference, you can decide the better financial path for you.

Be wary of car dealerships offering you an amount for your trade significantly greater than the actual value. Also, you will occasionally see or hear advertising guaranteeing a specific trade value for your vehicle no matter what. Either way, this process is called an over-allowance. Car dealerships are a for-profit organization, so any type of deal they are offering needs to make a profit somewhere down the line, which generally means it will cost you more money one way or the other.

Knowledge Drop

Henry Ford introduced the Ford Model T automobile and revolutionized transportation and manufacturing in the United States. Production line efficiency was so important, he famously said, "Any customer can have a car painted any color that he wants, so long as it is black."

Here is how an over-allowance situation works. Let us assume your current vehicle has a trade-in value of $5,000 and you want to trade it in toward a new vehicle purchase of $25,000. You are ecstatic when the car dealership offers you $9,000 for your trade in. Well, because your car is only worth $5,000 to them, there is no way they can sell it for a profit if it costs them $9,000 to buy it from you. Therefore, they take the extra money they are offering you ($9,000 - $5,000 = $4,000), which is the over-allowance, and add it to the price of the new car you are buying. Even though they offered you more for your trade, their additional cost of $4,000 is added to your new car, making your purchase $29,000 instead of $25,000. If you aren't paying attention to the numbers, they can sneak this extra cost in without you even recognizing it.

This can also happen when you have a trade-in vehicle that has negative equity. Negative equity happens when your car's current value is less than what you owe on the loan. Negative equity can happen if you overpay for a vehicle, or the loan terms are so long the vehicle devalues quicker than you can pay it down. Let's assume that your car has a trade-in value of $5,000, but your current loan has a payoff value of $7,000. You have a negative equity of $2,000. To get the new car sale, dealerships will commonly use the negative equity as an over-allowance and add it to the new car sale. They pay off your current car for you at $7,000 and add the $2,000 over-allowance to the cost of the new car, increasing the new car cost from $25,000 to $27,000. In this case, you will still be paying for a car you no longer own. That is why it's so important to make a down payment plus research and negotiate good pricing and terms when you purchase a car, because the cost can negatively impact you in several different ways.

The best process is to negotiate the price of the new car and your trade in car independently of each other, so you know you are getting a reasonable deal on both.

Almost Done

After you have done all the hard work of researching and negotiating, the last step in the car buying process is being put in the dealership's F&I (Finance and Insurance) Manager's office, so don't let your guard down quite yet. This manager's responsibility includes completing your credit checks, loan documents, taking your down payment, and reviewing the terms of the purchase agreement. This is also a place where the dealership will try to sell you "extras" with various sales tactics. Know that these extra products and services generally come at a high markup for the dealership because they are holding you captive within the dealership at a time when you are most vulnerable. You are excited about driving your new car *and* you think you are done negotiating!

These "extras" can include life insurance for the car loan, extended warranty, gap insurance, and special maintenance packages. To combat the sales tactics, just practice the following response to each item, "No, thank you." Let's practice together – "No, thank you." You may have to say it multiple times but be patient, be respectful, and stand firm.

Of the extras I listed, the only two that *may* be worthwhile – based on your financial situation – are the life insurance for the loan and the gap insurance. As discussed earlier, if you need these items, go ahead and purchase them, but not from the car dealership, where they are offered at a higher cost.

Finally – You have a New Car

Now that all the negotiating and paperwork are done, you get to drive your new car home and enjoy it. But there are still a few things to keep in mind about your new purchase and how to protect and maintain your asset. First, your car will come with some sort of warranty. Review the details and take the car back to the dealership for any warranty or recall issues. After your car warranty has expired, find a non-dealership shop to complete all your needed maintenance. The parts and labor rates at a car dealership can be significantly higher than those at independent shops. As long as you find a reputable shop, use them for all non-warranty related repairs.

Secondly, read the owner's manual and maintenance schedule for your new car. These booklets will help you understand all the features of your new car and tell you how to maintain it. Be sure to follow all the recommended maintenance intervals for your vehicle or it could void the warranty on your vehicle and cause damage to the car.

At a bare minimum, be sure to change your oil, oil filter, and air filters according to the car's maintenance schedule, check the tire pressure at least once a month, and wax your car twice per year. One of the biggest factors in keeping your car's engine healthy is to change the oil as directed. Most cars have reminders built in to help you remember and follow the required schedule. Be sure to change the oil at the intervals recommended using the oil detailed in your owner's manual. Many quick lube oil change locations will try to dupe you into changing your oil every 3,000 miles, which is fine if that is what your owner's manual details, but most newer cars now have longer interval requirements.

Car tires are easy to maintain and easy to ruin. Not maintaining your tires properly will cost you a lot of money to replace or become a safety issue.

The best way to maintain your tires is to ensure they're inflated to the proper pressure. Go to your local hardware store or big box store and buy a reasonably priced tire pressure gauge. Open your driver's side door and look for a label attached inside the door edge. This label will detail the PSI (pounds per square inch) requirements for each tire. Many newer model cars will identify your tire pressures on a screen within the car, but if yours doesn't, you can manually check the tire pressures. Do this monthly, when there has been a big temperature change between seasons, or if you are driving through various climates. Adjust the tire pressures accordingly using the tire pressure gauge. Do *not* base it off the look of the tire, because it can be deceiving.

Tires improperly inflated cause heat, which can cause a tire to fail. Overinflated tires are just as bad as underinflated tires, so be sure you use a tire gauge to properly inflate them. One of the worst things that can happen is for a tire to fail while driving 75 miles per hour down an interstate. This could cause you to lose control of the vehicle or cause damage to the car because of flying debris as the tire comes apart. Invest in a tire pressure gauge for less than $10 and always keep it in your vehicle so you can check your tire pressure regularly.

If you ever find odd wear on any of your tires, have them inspected by a reputable tire service location to identify the problem. Tires are not only important for your safety; they can be expensive and require your attention to make sure you get good life out of them. A good practice is to rotate your tires to a different position on your car during every other oil change.

Lastly, take the time to put a coat of wax on your vehicle at least twice a year to keep the paint protected and looking good. In extreme environments or if your vehicle is parked outside of a garage, you should consider waxing your car four times per year.

As an overview, here is a list of car ownership top tips:

- Research the vehicle and pricing beforehand.
- Know the value of your trade-in.
- Get competitive financing quotes.
- Know when to walk away from a bad deal.
- Don't buy extras like life insurance, gap insurance, and extended warranty at the time of sale without research.
- Don't finance negative equity.
- Keep up with regular maintenance.
- Don't disregard recalls.
- Stay away from car dealership maintenance after the warranty period.

Chapter 30

Home Sweet Home

More than likely, the most expensive purchase you will ever make in your life is for a house. Also, because they're so expensive, a home purchase could easily be the most important purchase of your life. Whether you are a first-time home buyer or upgrading to a bigger house to accommodate a growing family, a new home is very exciting and can be an excellent investment.

Unlike a car, purchasing a home should allow you to get an ROI and build equity for your financial future. A home as an investment has similar attributes to other investments in the following ways:

- Home buying requires you to spend time on research to ensure you are making the best use of your money.
- Expect your investment to vary in value in the short term but increase in value over the long term.
- Homes should be considered a long-term investment.
- Homes, like other investments, need ongoing maintenance and attention to continue to be a good investment.

As investments, homes differ from other investments because they are not "liquid" or easily converted into cash. Unlike other financial investments including mutual funds, stocks, bonds, or savings accounts, homes are tangible, meaning you can touch them. They also do not see massive, daily swings in value like stocks or mutual funds can.

The information provided in this chapter focuses on buying a home to live in full time. This is not advice on buying a second home, buying a home to flip for a profit, or buying a home for the specific purpose of renting it out. All those purchases are riskier than a primary home purchase and should not be considered unless you have moved yourself toward the top of the Financial Pyramid. Do not use those strategies to move up the lower end of the Pyramid. Having a single house payment can be difficult enough during financially challenging times. Having more than one house payment at a time can cause significant strain on your finances during an economic downturn or catastrophic event that causes you to lose much-needed income.

Knowledge Drop

According to Statista, the U.S. home ownership rate in 2020 was 65.8%, which is up from 63.7% in 2016.

Any house you buy should have the opportunity to increase in value and give you a solid ROI. Preferably, this would be a free-standing home where you also own the land the home is built on. Condominiums and townhomes may be good investments in some circumstances but will not provide as good a long-term return as a house because you don't own the land it is built on. Also, a trailer is not a house. A trailer won't provide a good return and you should never buy one as a home or an investment.

A home can (and should) be part of your strategy to build wealth. You purchase a home to give you shelter and live your life, but at the same time you build equity to increase your wealth and move you up the Financial Pyramid.

Before You Buy

Before my wife and I purchased our first home, we bought and read a book called *Home Buying for Dummies*. It was probably one of the best purchases we have ever made. The "Dummies" books have a gift for taking a complicated and overwhelming topic and putting them into terms that are easy to understand. After you read my book completely and recommend it to five of your friends, go out and buy *Home Buying for Dummies* to help you understand the home buying process a bit better.

The more work you put into the home buying process before you buy a house, the less strain and frustration you will experience during and after the process is over. Home buying can be emotional and overwhelming, so spend time to inform yourself about how it works. That way, you can focus in on the details of your new home.

> **Knowledge Drop**
>
> According to Wikipedia, the Dummies series has more than 200 million books in print and around 2,500 titles. The topics are broad and offers something for everyone such as Accounting, Beekeeping and Ventriloquism.

Renting vs. Buying

Most people start out renting an apartment or home, sometimes by themselves and other times with roommates to make it more affordable. Renting has some significant advantages. Renting is a relatively short-term relationship. Rental agreements can vary from a month to a year, and you can decide to move out with little or no notice, or stay at the same place for a longer period of time. You have the flexibility to move to a new neighborhood, city, or state without having the worry of selling a house to someone else before you can move. You just pick up and leave.

When you rent, you have a landlord that fixes things when they break. You do not have to worry about fixing minor issues like a leaky faucet or shelling out cash to fix major issues, such as replacing the air conditioning or hot water heater. Renting gives you peace of mind. Related to that, it is easier to budget your housing expense because your costs will not fluctuate substantially like they can with home ownership, because all your maintenance costs are handled by your landlord.

As a renter, you also need to be aware of rent hikes at the end of your lease or being forced to move because the owner of the property is selling to a new owner who does not want a renter.

The overall cost of renting can be less than owning a home, due to the upfront costs, home loan payments, and ongoing maintenance and repairs. However, owning a home may give you some tax advantages by being able to deduct mortgage interest expenses and property taxes.

Plus, home ownership gives you something renting does not – equity. As your home appreciates in value and you pay off any mortgage associated with it, your equity will grow. Increased equity means increased wealth, and that moves you up the Financial Pyramid.

Most people want to eventually move away from renting and buy a home of their own. It is part of the process we like to call adulting. Not only do you get tired of cramped apartments with noisy neighbors, but you want to get something in return for that monthly payment. Why not use that money for an investment where you can get a return instead of lining someone else's pockets? If you have worked hard on your financial health and put yourself in a reasonable position to buy a house, then read on.

The Math: How Much House Can You Afford

Back in 1999, we went through the process of buying our first home. After we had done our research and educated ourselves about the home buying process, we went through the steps of getting pre-approved for a home loan. Just like today, by getting pre-approved for a loan, you are showing a potential seller that you are a qualified buyer with the funding to potentially buy their house. This can be critical during times when home buying is competitive, meaning there is a housing shortage, or a particular house is highly sought after. If sellers have multiple offers for their house, they will pick the offer most advantageous to them, which will include ensuring that a potential buyer is qualified for a loan and the purchase will go through with no issues.

Anyway, during this initial process we had decided we could afford no more than $150,000 for a new home. The bank pre-approved us for over twice that number. They told us that if we wanted to get a loan for over $300,000, we could have it, even though we were only comfortable with $150,000. When the banker told us this news, all I could do was laugh because I honestly thought he was joking. I may or may not have offended him with my response, but it was simply ludicrous.

Knowledge Drop

According to the latest U.S. Census Bureau's American Housing Survey, the average mortgage payment on a 30-year fixed loan is $1,275.

After doing the math, a $300,000 loan would have taken every single bit of spare income we had to make payments. That meant no vacations, no splurge purchases, no retirement, no money for maintenance, and certainly no buffer if for some reason we lost our income. Needless to say, we bought our first home for $144,500. That amount allowed us to buy a great investment (the house) and still do all the other things we wanted, including saving for retirement and taking nice vacations.

As a side note, about eight years after this happened, the United States fell into one of the worst financial crises it had seen since the Great Depression. That period was dubbed the Great Recession. What was one of the primary causes of the Great Recession? Banks providing mortgages to people that could not afford them. Huh. Weird.

It's your responsibility to understand how much you can afford for a new loan – not the loan officer, not the bank, not a real estate agent, not your neighbors – you! The best way you can figure this out is by following the tips in this book that include creating and following a budget, paying bills on time, establishing your uh-oh fund, and building your savings account in case you lose your income for a longer stretch of time. Leave yourself a buffer and don't spend every single available dollar on your mortgage payment. That is called being house poor, and it can be financially devastating. Not only are you unable to defer the proper amount of money toward savings and your retirement accounts, if something bad happens, you have no ability to sustain a long-term loss of income. This can result in bankruptcy and possibly even losing your home.

> **Money Decree**
>
> Do not buy what you can afford – buy less.

To qualify for a mortgage, banks and sometimes real estate agents will use formulas based on your income to determine how much you can "afford." This is all fine and dandy except there is a key aspect they are leaving out: how much of your income you already spend.

Did I say that it's your responsibility to understand how much you can afford for a new loan? Don't rely on anyone else or some random formula to determine your loan amount because you are the one taking on the responsibility of those monthly mortgage payments.

Whatever you think you can afford, buy less. Living below your means saves a lot of grief and financial stress down the road.

Some More Math: A House Costs More Than Just a Mortgage Payment

Remember that time you were searching for a hotel room and a website claimed a rate of $125 per night, but it actually costs you $175 per night after fees and taxes? Buying a house can be like that, so know what you're getting yourself into.

Beyond a mortgage payment there are several other factors to consider when budgeting for the purchase of a home and the ongoing costs after you buy.

In the next section, we'll dig deeper into how mortgage payments can be specifically structured but let's look at all the other factors first.

- **Appraisal:** After you make an offer on a house, banks will require you to get an appraisal of the house you want to buy. An expert will review the home in detail to understand the market value to ensure the amount you are paying for a home is in line with the current market conditions. For example, a bank does not want to loan you $500,000 for a house only worth $300,000. Why? Because if you default on the loan, the bank will take possession of the house and sell it to someone else so they can recoup their costs. If the home is worth less than the loan amount, it's tougher for the bank to get their money back.

Knowledge Drop

The hotel industry raked in an estimated $2.9 billion in revenue related to resort fees, and other fees and surcharges in 2018, according to Bjorn Hanson, Ph.D., a hotel consultant and clinical adjunct professor at New York University.

- **Home inspection:** Along with the appraisal, you will also pay a qualified home inspector to look at the home before the purchase takes place to ensure there are no structural issues, building code violations, or safety issues with the home. This protects you and the bank from buying a home with structural or maintenance issues that could be costly down the road. No house is perfect, but the home inspection will allow you to decide if there are any major issues to be repaired before the purchase can go through, or the inspectors report could allow you to back out of the deal altogether.

  In some situations, you may be enticed to waive the home inspection during negotiations. This is a bad idea. The house is a considerable investment, and you should complete all the due diligence to make sure you are getting what you pay for.
- **Closing costs:** The act of buying a house is expensive and the closing costs (the costs associated with the purchase) can be thousands of dollars. Beyond the appraisal and home inspections, other costs can include, but are not limited to:

- o Fees from your lender for creating your loan, including origination fees, which are fees charged by the lender that add to their profit from the loan.
- o Fees charged by the escrow company for taxes and title-related expenses.
- o Transition expenses between owners. If you buy a home in the middle of the month, the owner could have paid monthly costs for the home that include HOA fees or property taxes that you need to pay back to the seller.
- o Initial escrow balances. Mortgage companies will include the cost of your homeowner's insurance and property taxes into your monthly mortgage payment and pay them on your behalf on their due date. When you buy a house, you must pay money into an escrow account so there is an original balance to pay these costs when they come due.

> **Knowledge Drop**
>
> According to Nerdwallet and various other sources, closing costs average between 2% to 5% of the loan cost.

- ➢ **Private mortgage insurance (PMI):** If you purchase a home with less than a twenty percent down payment, the mortgage company will require you to purchase private mortgage insurance. PMI protects the lender in case you default on the loan and is consolidated with your monthly mortgage payment. Once you achieve over twenty percent equity in the home, which you can prove through another home appraisal, the bank will lift the PMI charges from your monthly payment.
- ➢ **Homeowner's insurance:** Insurance on your home is a must and is required by lenders to protect the investment. Along with your mortgage payment, they can have you make monthly payments into your mortgage escrow account that will cover your insurance premium.
- ➢ **Property taxes:** Most states have some sort of property tax liability based on the value of your property. To ensure you make the property taxes while you have a mortgage, a

portion of your monthly payment will be put into your escrow account to pay for the property taxes when they are due.

- **Homeowner's association dues (HOA):** Many communities in cities have HOAs, which is an organization that oversees the housing community you live in. They ensure homes and properties are maintained to certain standards to protect the value of the properties within the communities. You pay dues for the management of the community and for maintenance of common areas within the community, such as pools, parks, or greenbelts. If you live in a condominium, the HOA fees may also cover costs for the exterior of the condo along with garbage, sewer, and some utilities. Ensure you review the rules of the HOA and fees related to living in the community.
- **Maintenance:** There are two types of maintenance you should prepare for. The first is the unplanned events like a broken refrigerator, a leaking hot water heater, or an air conditioning system failure. The second is the planned maintenance like painting your home, upgrading the interior, or replacing your roof. Either way, repairs on a home can be expensive, especially if you ignore ongoing maintenance. Protect your investment by keeping up with repairs and maintaining things around your house before they break unexpectedly.

Occasionally when you purchase a home you can negotiate with the seller to buy a home warranty policy for a year after the purchase is complete. A home warranty is basically an insurance plan to cover the cost of repair or replacement of systems and appliances within the home. This can protect you from having to cover large expenses if something were to break.

Home warranties are good solutions in some scenarios but understand the companies supplying these "warranties" are for-profit organizations. They will work hard to repair instead of replacing failed systems or appliances no matter how old they are. Also, the service may not be the best. We have waited days to have an air conditioner fixed in the middle of the summer because the home warranty company wanted to save expense by hiring the cheapest company for repairs.

When you own a home, you should plan on repairing the minor things yourself. A simple internet search will train you on how to repair or replace anything from a ceiling fan to a leaky faucet and everything in between. Get yourself a good set of tools and have at it. But also understand your limitations. There are certain times you should hire a paid professional to ensure repairs are done properly and safely. It is a good idea to hire a professional for structural and electrical repairs unless you have a particular expertise in those areas.

To help recoup some costs of homeownership and entice people to own their homes, costs such as property taxes, PMI, and mortgage interest may be tax deductible. Tax law is fluid, so you need to do some research or talk to a tax advisor to see if you can take advantage of these benefits.

All About the Mortgage

Your home mortgage will be the biggest loan you will ever have, which means you need to know the ins and outs to ensure it does not cost you more than intended. Most common mortgages are structured for thirty years, but you can pretty much create your loan with any term limit you want up to thirty years. We refinanced a loan once to get a lower interest rate and got a term of 22 years, which was the amount of time we had left on our original loan before we refinanced. The lower the term of the loan, the lower the interest rate.

> **Knowledge Drop**
>
> The word "Mortgage" is derived from an old French term meaning "Death Pledge." So good luck with that.

Because your mortgage is a lot of money, the interest rate and length of the loan are critical to understand. To provide a visual of how the interest rate and term can impact costs, let's pretend you are buying a home and financing $400,000. Here are three examples to review:

Example	Interest Rate	Term (Years)	Monthly Payment	Total Interest Paid
A	5%	30	$2,147	$373,023
B	4%	30	$1,910	$287,478
C	4%	15	$2,959	$132,575

Example A is for a thirty-year loan at an interest rate of five percent. This loan will cost you $373,023 just in interest on the original $400,000 loan. Interest rates fluctuate dramatically according to several factors, but when you consider borrowing money for only five percent you would think that's a great deal. Even if it were a great deal, that five percent costs over $373,000 in interest – almost as much as you borrowed in the first place. That is a huge number and hopefully proves the point that mortgages are expensive, and you need to pay attention to the details, not just the payment.

In example B, I lowered the interest rate from five percent to four percent and our interest decreased by over $85,000 for the term of the loan.

Example C shows the same interest rate of four percent, but the loan's term is lowered to fifteen years which causes the payment to increase considerably. Your interest cost is reduced by nearly $155,000 from the thirty-year loan at four percent interest and over $240,000 from the thirty-year loan at five percent. Could you use an extra $155,000 in your pocket? How about $240,000?

When you are ready to move forward with buying a house, find a good mortgage broker to help you identify mortgage terms that work for you and are competitive in the marketplace. A mortgage broker will do the work to get you qualified for the best rates with the banks. He or she will then provide you the best deals instead of you accepting bids from several banks yourself. Then you can review amortization schedules for each loan term and identify how much the loan will cost you.

As you begin dabbling in the wonderful world of mortgages, you'll find there are many different options where banks are trying to "help" you afford a new home. Remember our big picture – we want to build wealth and move up the Financial Pyramid. If you only focus on a mortgage payment and ignore all the terms making up that payment, you may find yourself in trouble. I would highly recommend sticking with a mortgage offering standard terms that include a fixed interest rate for the entire term of the loan. An alternative to a conventional loan is an adjustable-rate mortgage (ARM) which I recommend to stay away from.

Adjustable-rate mortgage (ARM): An ARM is just what it says. The rate can and will adjust over time. The premise with an ARM is to have an initial fixed, low interest rate for the first few years. Then, the rate can change based on the market conditions. The rate can change annually, quarterly, or even monthly based on the terms of your loan. So, when you create the loan, you literally will not know your payment amount after the initial term of the loan is completed.

> **Knowledge Drop**
>
> The Pew Research Institute found that 24 percent of American adults had not read a book, in part or whole, in the last year. Be proud that you are almost done with this one!

An ARM basically forces you to guess what mortgage rates will be doing three to five years from now. If the market has lower interest rates, then your ARM will go down, making your payment and interest costs decrease. If the market has higher interest rates, your ARM will go up, causing an increased payment and interest costs. Since none of us can ever tell the future of the market, steer away from these loans. If your rate goes up significantly after your first few years, you could be in a world of hurt because you may not be able to afford your new mortgage payment. As you have already seen, small movements in the interest rate can cost you a large amount of money.

Plain and simple, if you are wanting to use an ARM so a house payment is affordable to you, then you cannot afford the house.

Paying Points for A Lower Rate

One of the games, I mean opportunities, some banks will provide is to provide you a lower interest rate if you pay fees up front. These are called discount points. Basically, you write them a check that goes directly to their profit and in return you get a lower interest rate. Complete an analysis of the total cost of the loan that includes paying to reduce your interest rate and see if it is worth it. Generally it is not, and you should steer away from paying up-front fees to lower your interest rate.

The Down Payment – Do's and Don'ts

Before buying a house, you need to have your financial house in order, which includes having money for a down payment. The more you put down on a house, the more you can save in interest charges down the road. For example, if you were to put ten percent (or $40,000) down on a $400,000 house, your monthly payment would go from $1,910 to $1,719 and the total interest paid on the loan would decrease by almost $30,000 compared to no down payment at all.

Therefore, you should put as much down as you can afford with a goal of no less than ten percent when the time comes to buy a house. The higher the down payment, the better you will be seen from the bank's perspective because you will have some automatic equity built into the house and be less of a risk for them. Home prices fluctuate due to market conditions. Sometimes the housing market is hot, and pricing escalates; other times people aren't looking for new homes and home prices will stagnate or decrease. If you make a low down payment on your home and market conditions deteriorate, then it would be tough for you to sell your home because you may owe more money on it than its current value. That likelihood is decreased as your down payment increases, because you start out with equity in your home from day one.

The size of your down payment, along with other factors like your credit score, payment history, and income can also help you receive better overall loan terms.

When calculating the amount you are going to use for a down payment, also keep in mind that the money will no longer be "liquid," meaning easily accessible. When you deposit money in your checking or savings account you can withdraw it by going to the nearest ATM. That is liquid. When you put money toward a house, it is hard to access this cash and should be considered a long-term financial asset that you will not use for a long time.

Now for the don'ts. *Do not rob your uh-oh fund or retirement funds for a down payment on a house.* You will need the uh-oh fund in case something goes wrong with your house after you buy it, and your retirement funds are for retirement and nothing else.

If you have a 401k retirement plan at your workplace, one of the primary characteristics is that you can take out money from the 401k without penalty for a few specific reasons. One of those reasons is for a down payment on a house, but do *not* do it. You are robbing yourself of one long term investment for another and it doesn't make financial sense.

Refinancing

Refinancing a mortgage means you take your current mortgage and change it to a new one that includes updated terms for the interest rate and the length of the mortgage. You are basically wiping your current mortgage clean and creating a new one.

The state of the economy can drive mortgage interest rates up and down over time. Rates can move daily, but it is a good idea to keep a watchful eye on the general trend of mortgage rates in case they drop to a lower level than your current loan. Generally speaking, if the current rates are lower by one percent or more compared to your current rate, then a refinance may be a good idea. As we just discussed, anytime you get a new mortgage there are costs associated with it, so before you decide to refinance, do the math that includes closing costs and a new amortization schedule to see if it makes sense.

The goal of a refinance is to lower the overall cost you pay for a mortgage, not just to lower your payment. This is another scenario where you must look beyond lowering your payment and focus on the overall cost of your loan.

As we discussed in scenarios above, a one percent decrease in a mortgage interest rate can make a significant difference over time. However, refinancing can create some common pitfalls that can negate the overall benefit of refinancing. Now let's look at some do's and don'ts for refinancing.

DO refinance a loan if there is a cost savings to you due to a lower interest rate. A cost savings means your total loan cost is lowered, not just your payments. But **DO NOT** increase the term of the loan past your current loan.

Let's pretend you have 25 years left on a thirty-year mortgage and you determine the market is providing lower interest rates to your advantage. After refinancing, your new mortgage should not be any longer than 25 years. If you refinance your current 25-year loan to a new thirty-year loan, you are actually paying off your loan in 35-years (five years you have already paid, plus the new thirty-year loan).

Let's look at this scenario with actual numbers. You start with a thirty-year, $400,000 mortgage and a four percent interest rate. If you pay off this mortgage in thirty years, the total interest will be $287,478. However, after paying the mortgage for five years, the interest rate drops to three percent, so you will want to refinance in this case.

The first five years of the loan, you have already paid $77,576 in interest and the new loan balance is $361,086, which is the amount you refinance. If you refinance for 25 years at three percent, your interest charges for all thirty years will be $230,183, which is a savings of over $50,000 from your original loan.

If you refinance for another thirty years (instead of 25), the total interest charges for the 35 years you are paying the mortgage jumps to $264,537. This still saves you $24,000 from the original loan, but by creating another thirty years on top of the original five, you aren't taking full advantage of the savings.

Let's say in another five years, there is a benefit to refinance for a second time. If you refinance with another thirty-year loan, your payment will decrease again. However, you just pushed your loan term another five years down the road, which means it will now take you *forty* years to pay off that original thirty-year loan.

> **Knowledge Drop**
>
> Did you know that 58 percent of adults in America said they enjoyed their math class experiences in grades K-12, according to the Pew Research Institute? That means 42 percent of you stopped reading about one and a half pages ago.

I have seen people refinance numerous times with new thirty-year term mortgages because it decreases their payment even further, but it doesn't take full advantage of the lower interest rate, which is the point of refinancing. Lowering your mortgage payment is great, and I am all for it, but if you just keep pushing the end of your mortgage-paying years further and further down the road, you end up paying more and more interest. And this delay postpones how long it takes to build more equity in your home.

If you refinance multiple times, you could end up paying thirty-five, forty, or more years on the original thirty-year loan. And at what cost? I know a smaller payment is hard to pass up but look at the bigger picture – moving up the Financial Pyramid. Do not be so enticed by the short-term gain of a lower payment that you miss the bigger benefit of paying down your debt and increasing your equity.

So, the rule is you must keep the length of the loan the same *or less* than your current loan.

DO refinance your loan in a way that makes your new payment and current payment relatively the same. In this scenario, you reduce the term of the loan, so your payment is relatively the same as your current loan but with a lower interest rate. See the table below to understand this concept. The information shows how a refinance would work if you had a current thirty-year loan with a $300,000 balance and 25 years left.

	Term	Interest Rate	Payment	Total Interest Paid
Current Mortgage	25 Years Left	5%	$1,610.46	$226,131
Refinanced Mortgage	21 Years	4%	$1,614.88	$205,189

In this example your current payment is $1,610. By refinancing your loan to four percent and reducing your time of repayment from 25 years to 21 years, your payment is almost identical ($1,615). By getting a term that leaves your payments the same, you reduce your repayment by four years *and* the amount of interest decreases by over $20,000 during the length of the new loan.

Another common pitfall of refinancing is taking equity out of your home. **DO** refinance for the same amount or lower than your current mortgage. If you decide to refinance your mortgage, the new mortgage should finance no more than your current principal. Too many times, people will refinance their mortgage for the sole purpose of getting additional cash to compensate for uncontrolled spending in their lives. Here is how it works. You have a 25-year mortgage with $300,000 left to pay, but your house is worth $400,000. You take out a $400,000 mortgage, use $300,000 to pay off your current mortgage and the other $100,000 is given to you as a cash payment. If you use that money for everyday expenses, just know you are now paying finance charges on that spending, because it is included in your mortgage cost. In this example, you have removed all the equity from your home to offset expenses in your household. However, this strategy *may* make sense if you are using the funds to improve the value of your home through a remodel or improvement. **DO NOT** refinance to remove equity from your home unless you need money in an extreme emergency, or you are using the equity to improve the value of your home.

Recently, my wife and I considered buying a new home. While investigating the home's value and history, our real estate agent saw in the current owner's records that they refinanced the house three times over the last four years. They continued to take equity out every time equity was available. My response was that they were probably in financial trouble. The real estate agent's response was, "Well, it's expensive to live here!" When you continually use your home's equity to pay your ongoing expenses, you should take a good hard look at your expenses and the house you live in. It could very well be that you cannot afford either one.

> **Knowledge Drop**
>
> Our current national debt is over $28 trillion. If you were to stack 28 trillion $1 bills, it would be tall enough to make 4 round trips to the moon.

Unless the cash is used for an emergency, this practice is not a sound financial decision, it does not build wealth, and it does not move you up the Financial Pyramid.

Paying Off Your Mortgage Early

Beyond a refinanced mortgage, another way to save interest costs on your mortgage is to pay it down early. A traditional mortgage should allow you to pay off your mortgage whenever you want without penalty. If you can put additional money toward your mortgage – either occasionally or continually – the financial impact can be significant. Looking at the size and time of your current mortgage can be daunting but take it in baby steps and any additional amounts paid will help you in the long run.

There are various strategies to pay down your mortgage early. One way is to consider how your paychecks match up to your mortgage payments. Many employees get paid every two weeks. This means that ten months of the year you get two paychecks, and two months of the year you get three paychecks. What if you take that third paycheck and pay down your mortgage?

Another way to pay down your mortgage is to use any unexpected money or windfall. Did you get a tax refund? How about a bonus at work? Did your long-lost great uncle on your dad's side pass away and leave you an inheritance? How about using half of the unexpected windfall to pay down your mortgage instead of going on a spending spree?

Or you can simply pay $10, $20, or $50 extra per month toward paying down your loan.

I have a couple of rules about the process of paying down your mortgage. First, make sure to pay down the principal instead of making extra payments. Remember that when you make a payment to the mortgage company it encompasses costs for the principal, interest, PMI, homeowner's insurance, and property taxes. If you are trying to pay down your mortgage with extra money, you only want the money to go toward the principal. By reducing the principal, you automatically reduce the interest costs.

There was a time when we started paying our mortgage down early on a continuous basis. We sent extra money each month to start reducing the principal. I would make the payment by check and on the payment slip I would note how much was for our regular payment and how much was to pay down the principal. After a couple months of doing this, I signed into our account to look at the mortgage balance and noticed the bank was not applying the extra money to the principal. They were applying it as another payment or portion of a payment, which meant some of our money went toward interest charges.

I called them to apply the money properly and they did. The next month, I wrote how much should be applied to the principal on the payment slip, AND on the check, AND with a sticky note attached to the check. And guess what? They made the same mistake again. If I did not check my account, I would have never known. The lesson here is to be sure it gets applied correctly because mistakes happen.

The second rule of paying down your mortgage is not to pay the bank anything extra to pay off your mortgage early. I have seen programs where you can pay a bank an additional fee to make your payments every two weeks to align with your payroll checks, instead of making a payment once per month. This scenario is a double whammy. First, you are paying extra money to the bank when you can do it yourself for free. Second, your payments may not be going directly to reducing your principal as we just discussed. If you have extra cash to go toward your mortgage, then just do it yourself and apply it toward your principal.

How big of a deal is it to pay off your mortgage early? Assume you have 25 years left on your mortgage with a current principal balance of $300,000 at a four percent interest rate. If you pay it out "as is" without any additional payments, you will pay over $175,000 in interest. If you pay $100 per month extra, your interest paid will drop to $156,000. I don't know about you, but that $19,000 difference seems like a big deal to me.

Which House to Buy

There are many things to consider when you look at homes to buy. Obviously from a financial perspective, you want to buy a home most likely to increase in value over time, and the biggest thing to consider is location. While evaluating a neighborhood or a specific home, consider the following questions:

- Does the community look inviting and how is the appearance of the homes? What were your first impressions when you entered the community?

- Does an HOA help manage the community? Sometimes people get upset by HOA rules, but they help maintain the look and feel of a community. I love the color purple, but I would not want my neighbor to paint their house purple. Sometimes rules are good.
- If you are looking at a specific home, are the neighbors' homes kept up well? You cannot choose your neighbors and they can change over time, but it is something to consider.
- How close are the schools? Even though you may not have kids now, you could someday, or sell the house to someone who does.
- How much traffic is near or in front of the house? If there are speed bumps within your community, there's a reason why. That doesn't mean you shouldn't buy the house; it just means you should understand the traffic patterns and be prepared to deal with them.
- Does your home back up to a busy road? We owned a home where commercial businesses, including a gas station, were on the other side of the wall. There were trees along the back fence that dampened some of the noise, but you could certainly hear the noise from our backyard or upstairs bedroom.
- Does your home back up to an industrial area? Understand that some industrial areas may operate all night long, which could produce unpleasant noise while you're trying to sleep.
- Is the community or house close to an area that could create loud noise or bad traffic patterns? These could include an airport, train tracks, a highway, or a sporting event facility.

Finding the right house can be nerve wracking and emotional. Just know that it can take some time to find what you want, so be patient and stay within your budget.

Selling Your Home

Eventually, you will need to sell your home. Maybe you were offered a new job in a new city, you need a larger home because your family is expanding, or you are downsizing because your kids moved out on their own. There are lots of factors to consider when selling your home, but from a financial perspective I want to focus only on one. Put your home on the open market where you have a greater opportunity for competitive offers. Because we live in a society where we demand immediate gratification, companies are popping up that will pay you cash for your home relatively simply and quickly.

If offers are too good to be true, they probably are. This is your largest financial asset; do you really want to rush through a transaction just so you can get paid quicker? Treat your asset with respect and go through the process of prepping your asset for sale and understand the full value of it. Those companies that dangle cash in front of you with the promise of a quick transaction are taking advantage of you. They will offer a price below market value for your home because they are offering you immediate cash. That cash comes at a price, at your expense.

Put your home on the open market and get paid what your property is worth. Is it harder? Absolutely. Is it worth it? Absolutely.

The Last Chapter

Only Those with Goals Achieve Them

Well – there you go. I have just provided you a long list of suggestions, tips, knowledge, hacks, and information that can help you build a foundation for your financial success. What now?

First, have a little celebration. You just finished reading a book and we need to do a better job of celebrating those small accomplishments in life.

Secondly, set some goals for yourself. Create a small financial goal to complete tomorrow. Skip your daily overpriced latte. Eat at home, instead of at a restaurant. It doesn't matter the goal, just that you set it and work toward it.

Then, set a goal to accomplish over the next week. Create your first steps toward building a budget or creating your uh-oh fund by identifying your number required and where you will store the money.

Next, set a goal to accomplish by the end of the month. These small steps add up to big things. Small financial changes should be acknowledged and celebrated – but not by spending money. Reward yourself: watch your favorite TV show, eat your favorite meal, or have your favorite drink.

Other short-term goals you could consider are:

- Establish regular and automatic transfers into a savings account for your uh-oh fund.
- If you aren't already, start contributing to your employer's 401k plan. If you currently participate, increase your contribution by at least one percent or to an amount to take full advantage of the matching program.
- If you have more than two credit cards, decide which have the best features and only use those moving forward.
- Review your insurance plans to ensure you have proper coverage at a competitive price.
- Begin following a budget today.
- Read one financial blog a week and one financial book a month to learn something new about personal finance.

After you have some short-term and relatively easy goals and accomplishments under your belt, think about some bigger picture goals. Four weeks from now, I want you to make a list of goals that are least a year out. Below is a list of what those goals could look like. But make sure you tailor these toward your own situation and how you want to live your life. Do not just steal this list and call them your own. This list is just to get your mind working.

Money Decree

Financial independence is achieved by the size of your wealth, not your income.

Longer Term Goals

- Fully fund my uh-oh fund in 18 months.
- Identify three expenses in my budget to reduce or eliminate by the end of the year.
- Reduce my credit card debt by half in twelve months and eliminate it in 24 months.
- Become debt free by the age of forty.

- In the next two years, move up at least one step in the Financial Pyramid.

Reading, planning, and learning about financial topics are all fine and dandy, but that's the easy part. Success all comes down to you. The success comes to those who are committed and work hard toward their goal. And that is the hard part. But here is my belief in humans: when we put our minds to something, we can and will accomplish anything. And anything worthwhile takes hard work to get there.

You have spent the time and energy to educate yourself by reading this book. Now keep that momentum going and establish some goals and action items to move up the Financial Pyramid. If you put your mind to it, you will accomplish it.

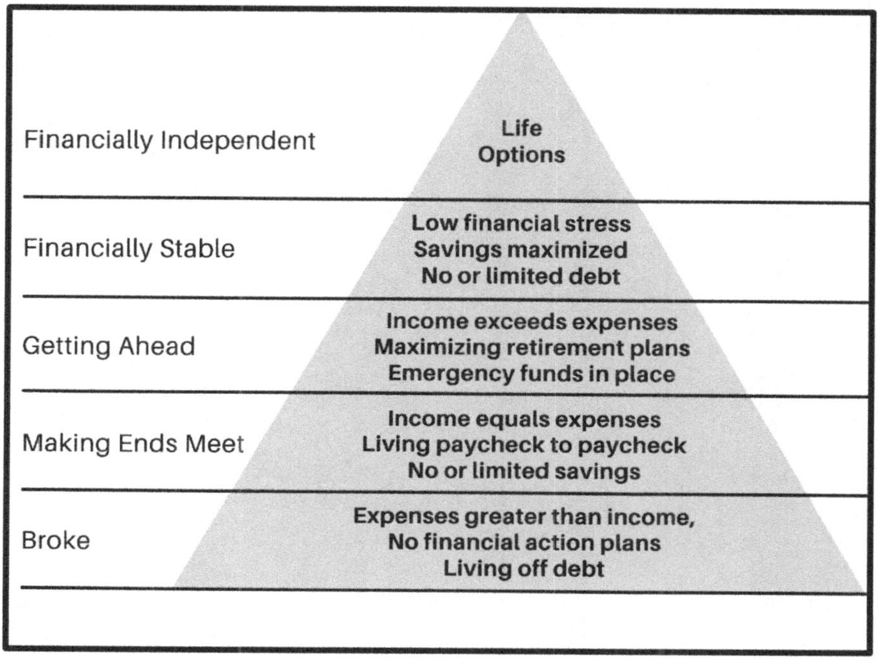

PART V

A BUNCH OF HELPFUL LISTS

Financial Calendar of Events

Here is a list of financial action items that should take place over a year. Use this list to put reminders in your calendar so you receive automatic notifications to complete each task.

- Weekly (at a minimum): Enter receipts in money program
- Monthly:
  - Compare last month's budget with actual results
  - Bank statement reconciliations
  - Credit card statement reconciliations
  - Review credit score reported by your credit card
- Annually:
  - Review car insurance quotes
  - Review home insurance quotes
- January 1
  - Compare last year's budget with actual results
  - Make money resolutions for coming year
  - Adjust 401k contributions, as needed
  - Adjust IRA contributions, as needed
  - Review current net worth
  - Review annual credit report on Experian
  - Review performance of your investments
  - Check your short-term savings accounts for competitive interest rates
- February 1: Start collecting tax documents and begin completing your taxes
- March 1:
  - Complete taxes
  - Update W4 tax withholding, as needed, based on tax results
- April 1: Review performance of your investments
- April 15 (at the latest): File taxes
- May 1: Review annual credit report on TransUnion
- July 1:
  - Review current net worth
  - Review performance of your investments

    - Check your short-term savings accounts for competitive interest rates
- September 1: Review annual credit report on Equifax
- October 1: Review performance of your investments
- November 1: Review end-of-year tax action items like utilizing tax credits
- December 1: Complete next year's budget

Dad's Money Decrees

- Building wealth is a series of small, disciplined decisions.
- Put an emphasis on experiences instead of material things.
- Do not buy into get rich quick schemes. Buying a lottery ticket is not a retirement plan.
- Most people who want to be millionaires, *actually* mean they want to *spend* a million dollars, which is the exact opposite of being a millionaire.
- Do not worry about what others have or buy.
- Just because a product or service is more expensive doesn't guarantee it is better.
- Money is not an infinite resource. Treat it with respect.
- Spend with a plan and purpose in mind.
- One of the hardest things about having money is not spending it.
- Earn job promotions and raises, do not just expect them.
- Take responsibility for your financial future. Do not depend on family, friends, or the government.
- Living below your means, means living without short term wants.
- You are in charge of protecting your money, because no one else will.
- Building wealth is not a competition.
- Budget and track every single dollar you make and spend.
- Do not buy what you can afford – buy less.
- Financial independence is achieved by the size of your wealth, not your income.

Accounts Financially Savvy People Should Own

- Checking account
- Bank savings account
- High yield savings account
- Money market
- 401k retirement plan or equivalent
- IRA – Individual Retirement Account
- Taxable retirement account / brokerage account

The list of other accounts that should be considered:

- CDs – Certificate of Deposit
- 529 plan
- HSA – Health Savings Account or HRA – Health Reimbursement Arrangement

PART VI

DEFINITIONS

401k matching Many employers will contribute money to your 401k or match a certain amount of money you invest as a benefit of working for them.

401k retirement plan This is a type of retirement plan offered by many employers. The plan allows you to take pre-tax dollars from your paycheck and invest it for the purpose of retiring.

529 plan A tax advantaged account that can be used to pay for qualified education related costs.

ARM – Adjustable-rate mortgage This mortgage will have a low fixed rate for the first few years of the loan and fluctuate based on market conditions after the initial period.

Amortization schedule A table showing loan payments over time with details about how much each payment is applied to principal and interest until it is completely paid off.

Asset A resource with a financial value.

ACH – Automated Clearing House A type of secure and convenient way to transfer money from one bank account to another.

Beneficiary A person designated by you to receive money from a specific account when you die.

Capitalized cost In a car lease, this is the difference between the sales price and the residual value of the car. It determines the amount financed and ultimately your lease payment amount.

Catch-up contributions Increased contribution limits to a tax deferred retirement plan available to older workers.

Car leasing A way to finance the use of a new car where you rent the car for a defined period with restrictions on mileage.

Closing Costs Expenses paid at the time of closing for the purchase of a house, not including the down payment.

Collections If you owe a company money and do not repay it within the stated time frame, the company may hire a third-party business to collect the money on their behalf.

College tuition reimbursement benefit Payment of college tuition by an employer to an employee under certain guidelines. Some employers offer this as a benefit to their employees.

Credit report A statement that provides your history of credit, including how much debt you have and how well you meet payment terms.

Credit score A number produced by credit bureaus that identifies your overall creditworthiness. Credit scores range from 300 to 850 with a higher number representing a better credit risk to a borrower.

Deductible This is an amount of money you must pay before your insurance company will start helping you pay bills. Health insurance deductibles are based on an annual basis, others are on a per incident basis.

Dental insurance Insurance to pay for visits to the dentist or dental emergencies.

Direct deposit An amount of money automatically deposited into your account(s).

Down payment An amount of cash paid up front by a person getting a loan to pay for a portion of a purchase before the remaining balance is financed with a loan.

Equity The difference between the current value of an asset minus any debt associated with the asset.

FDIC Insurance The FDIC (Federal Deposit Insurance Corporation) is an independent agency of the United States government that protects you against the loss of your insured deposits if an FDIC-insured bank or savings association fails. FDIC insurance is backed by the full faith and credit of the United States government.

Federal Tax Returns A form or forms filed with the federal government determining your taxable income, amount of tax paid, and the amount of tax due each year.

FICA The United States federal payroll tax. It stands for the Federal Insurance Contributions Act.

FICO score A brand name of a type of credit score named after the Fair Isaac Corporation.

Financially independent A person or family who has achieved all or most of their financial goals and no longer needs a consistent paycheck for income.

Health insurance Insurance to protect you for health-related issues such as doctor's visits, medications, hospital visits, and emergency care for you and your family.

Health insurance co-insurance In a year's time, if you have met your required deductible amount, co-insurance kicks in. This is the amount you still need to pay after you exceed your deductible.

Health insurance co-payment This is an amount of money you must pay for an office visit with your primary doctor or specialist. Typically, these amounts will be printed on the insurance card you receive after you sign up for the health insurance.

HSA – Health Savings Account or HRA – Health Reimbursement Arrangements This account allows you to contribute pre-tax money to use for future medical expenses. These are becoming more common because deductibles (and therefore out of pocket expenses) have increased dramatically. The HSA gives you a way to save pre-tax money to compensate for the higher deductibles in your health plan.

High deductible health plan To help keep health insurance premiums low, some insurance plans offer a high deductible, which requires you to pay more money before your insurance company starts pitching in. Typically, these types of plans are accompanied with a Health Savings Account.

High Yield Savings account A type of savings account generally available with online banks which pays a significantly higher savings rates compared to traditional banks.

Home warranty A type of insurance to cover repair or replacement of many systems and appliances in your house.

Homeowner association dues Dues paid on a regular basis to a homeowner's association when you own a home within a community that has an HOA.

HOA – Homeowners Association A community organization that establishes and enforces standards and rules within the community. The primary benefit of an HOA is to maintain standards to help improve the value of your home.

Income Money received generally through paychecks from employment or investments.

Insurance premium Money paid to companies for insurance coverage.

Interest Money charged to you as a cost of borrowing money, or money received by you as a premium within a savings account.

Investments A purchased asset with the assumption it will generate income or appreciate in value.

IRA – Individual Retirement Account An investment account used for retirement savings that appreciates tax-free or tax-deferred.

Life insurance Insurance that is paid to a loved one in case you die.

Long-term disability Insurance paid over a period of weeks or months to compensate for lost income in case you cannot work for various reasons.

Medicare This is an insurance program administered by the government. You pay money into the program through taxes, and you will be able to withdraw money from the program as soon as you meet eligibility requirements, such as age. The Medicare tax is a fixed percentage of your paychecks.

Minimum wage The minimum amount of wages required by law to be paid to workers.

Minimum payment (on credit cards) Credit card companies will provide you a minimum payment amount on your monthly statement generally representing only 1% to 3% of the balance on your card.

Money market An investment account similar to savings accounts except with slightly more risk and no FDIC insurance.

Mortgage A loan to purchase a home where the lender will take possession of the home in case of default.

Mortgage discount points Upfront fees paid by you to a mortgage company to get a lower interest rate on a loan.

Mortgage escrow account An account where a portion of your monthly mortgage payment will be held to pay for property taxes and homeowner's insurance on your behalf.

MSRP – Manufacturer's Standard Retail Price A standard price set by a manufacturer as a recommended price for the product. In the case of a car, the MSRP is generally inflated and should never be used as the price of the vehicle.

Mutual fund A professionally managed investment fund that pools money from many investors and purchases stocks, bonds, money markets, and/or other assets on your behalf.

Net Worth The value of all your assets, minus your liabilities.

No-load mutual funds A mutual fund that does not charge any sales fees or commissions to buy or sell the mutual fund.

Origination Fee A fee charged by a bank to process a loan application.

Opportunity Cost The foregone benefit that would have been obtained by an option not chosen.

Over allowance A car dealership calculation where cost is added to a car purchase to make up for overpaying on a trade in vehicle.

PTO – Paid time off, vacation and/or sick days Pay made to employees for days when you are not at work while on vacation or if you are sick.

Pre-tax dollars The amount of your paycheck before it is reduced by income taxes.

Principal The amount of a loan that you originally borrowed and promised to pay back.

PMI – Private mortgage insurance An insurance policy required by mortgage lenders when a mortgage has less than 20% equity. This insurance helps protect the lender in case of default.

Property taxes Taxes charged by local governments usually based on the value of a property.

Residual cost A calculation used in car leasing to determine the value of the car at the end of a lease term.

ROI – Return on investment A ratio dividing the profit on an asset with the cost of an asset.

Short-term disability Insurance paid over a short period of time (a few weeks) to compensate for lost income in case you cannot work for various reasons.

Social Security This is an insurance program administered by the government. You pay money into the program through payroll taxes and you will be able to withdraw money from the program as soon as you meet eligibility requirements, such as age. This program is thought of by many as a "retirement plan," but that was not the purpose of the program, nor should you depend on it for all your retirement income. The tax is a fixed percentage of your paychecks.

State Tax Returns A form or forms filed with the state government determining your taxable income, amount of tax paid, and the amount of tax due each year.

Tax shelter A legal strategy to lower your income taxes.

Term life insurance An insurance policy that provides a lump sum amount of money to your beneficiaries when you die. The insurance is for a specific period with a fixed premium during the term of the insurance.

Venmo A mobile payment application that moves money from person to person by using an email address or cell number, or can be used to purchase goods or services. Venmo accounts have a digital wallet where you can send, receive, or hold funds and is linked to a bank account. Some transactions are charged a fee.

Vesting period or Vested The amount of time an employee must work for an employer to fully own employer contributions to the employee's retirement account.

Vision insurance Insurance to pay for visits to the eye doctor.

W2 A document provided by employers to the IRS and employees detailing wages paid and taxes withheld for a tax year. A W2 is used by the employee to file taxes each year.

W4 A document employees fill out to determine how much federal and state tax to withhold from their paychecks.

Wealth The amount of money and other assets a person possesses, generally measured by net worth.

Wellness programs To motivate employees to stay healthy, companies may offer discounts to gyms, training on healthy habits, and/or ways to stop smoking.

Zelle A free person-to-person mobile payment application that moves money directly from one bank account to another in a matter of minutes by using an email address or cell number.

Acknowledgements

Putting 70,000 words on paper is no easy task. Putting 70,000 words on paper about a topic that may be boring and dry to some is daunting. To make this book educational through a bit of entertainment was done by getting the help from many others. From the bottom of my heart, I say thank you:

To Bob and Betty Connors, Carri Andrews, and Tim Macuga for taking the time and effort to read the earlier versions of the book. I appreciate your honest opinions and feedback that helped me shape the voice and message. Thank you, thank you, thank you!

To Jessica Cornwell who was my editor for this book. I am grateful for her fresh perspective and professional guidance that helped me put the finishing touches on ***Things I Want My Kids to Know About Money***.

To Tanja Prokop of TLI Design who did an amazing job on this book cover. Thank you for your guidance and professionalism.

To Jen Iben, my lovely bride of 26+ years, who spent time reading and evaluating nearly every version of this book. Thank you for being my English teacher during this project (and the 30 years I have known you). I appreciate your advice, love, and support that gave me confidence to make this happen.

To Red and Jean Iben, my mother and father. Even though you are no longer here, you helped me write this book.

About the Author

Mike Iben is a self-described beer snob and financial tightwad who loves to crunch numbers. He grew up in a lower middle-class family in small-town Iowa, paid his own way through college, built a successful career, and eventually became a business owner. He retired at the age of 48 by using sound financial principles to build wealth. After his daughters were born, he had a near panic attack considering the overwhelming task of teaching his kids everything he knew about life...and money. He put his thoughts on paper, which became his first book, ***Things I Want My Kids to Know About Money***.

Made in the USA
Monee, IL
04 November 2026

67385930R10157